3-MINUTE
DEVOTIONS

from the Psalms

Inspiration for Women

© 2018 by Barbour Publishing, Inc.

Devotional writing by Vicki J. Kuyper in association with Snapdragon Groups, Tulsa, Oklahoma, USA.

Prayers by MariLee Parrish.

Print ISBN 978-1-68322-400-6

All scripture quotations are taken from the King James Version of the Bible.

Published by Barbour Books, an imprint of Barbour Publishing, Inc., 1810 Barbour Drive, Uhrichsville, Ohio 44683, www.barbourbooks.com

Our mission is to inspire the world with the life-changing message of the Bible.

Printed in the United States of America.

3-MINUTE DEVOTIONS

from the Psalms

Inspiration for Women

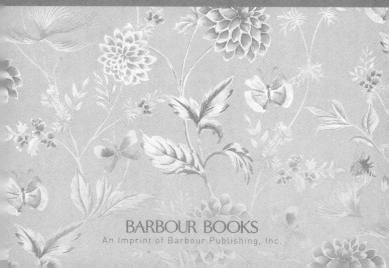

BARBOUR BOOKS
An Imprint of Barbour Publishing, Inc.

Introduction

As women, we can learn a lot about passion, emotion, and praise from the poetry of the book of Psalms. There were at least six authors—perhaps more—and they were nothing if not real. They cried out to God unabashedly, and their prayers seem to put our own struggles into words: *Where is God when I hurt? How can I forgive? Can I be forgiven? Are You really listening, God? Can I depend on You?*

Whether you're looking for an uplifting way to begin your day or seeking what the Bible has to say about a specific topic that's relevant to your life, *3-Minute Devotions from the Psalms: Inspiration for Women* is designed to help you draw near to the God who offers help, hope, and healing.

Say "Yes"

For the LORD God is a sun and shield: the LORD will give grace and glory: no good thing will he withhold from them that walk uprightly.

PSALM 84:11

You have a Father who owns the cattle on a thousand hills and holds the cosmos in His hands. This Almighty Father generously offers all He has to you. He offers you a life overflowing with joy, comfort, and blessing. But like any gift, this one has to be accepted before it can be enjoyed. Today, why not say yes to the Father who loves you? Tell Him how you long to live—and love—like His cherished child.

Yes, Father! I choose to trust You in times of plenty and in times when I have great need. I accept Your life and peace; this is what fills my heart with joy, comfort, and blessing even in the midst of difficulty.

The Abundant Life

Thou hast put gladness in my heart, more than in the time that their corn and their wine increased.

PSALM 4:7

An "abundant life" is not something we can pick up at the mall or purchase online. It comes from recognizing how much we receive from God each and every day. While some of our abundance may come in the form of possessions, the overflow of an abundant life ultimately comes from what fills our hearts, not our closets. Resting in God's "more-than-enough" can transform a desire to acquire into a prayer of thanksgiving for what we've already been given.

Your Word tells me that You fill me with joy in Your presence. Continue to put gladness in my heart, Lord. Show me how to be content with what You've given me.

8

God's Acceptance

The Lord hath heard my supplication;
the Lord will receive my prayer.

PSALM 6:9

People talk about "accepting" God into their lives. But it's God's acceptance of us that makes this possible. Because Jesus gave His life to pay the price for all the wrongs we've ever done, our perfect God can accept us wholeheartedly, even though we're far from perfect people. God not only accepts us, He also accepts our imperfect prayers. We don't have to worry about saying just the right words. The "perfect" prayer is simply sharing what's on our hearts.

Thank You that I didn't have to get all cleaned up before I could come to You, Jesus. I trust You to do the work in me to make me more like You day by day.

Free Gift

*I have hated them that regard lying
vanities: but I trust in the L*ORD.

PSALM 31:6

Religion is man-made, not God-made. Having a personal relationship with God is something totally different. It's not a list of rules and regulations or something we only "do" on Sundays. It's a love story between Father and child, a relationship in which we're totally accepted and unconditionally loved. Since we can't earn God's acceptance—it's a free gift of grace—that means we can't lose it either. God's acceptance releases us from the fear of rejection, so we're free to truly be ourselves.

I cannot fathom Your great gift, God. Thank You for bringing me freedom in Christ alone. Thank You for Your unfailing love for me. Show me how to love like that.

Joy of Living

---

*Thou hast also given me the shield of thy
salvation: and thy right hand hath holden me up,
and thy gentleness hath made me great.*

PSALM 18:35

Accomplishing something worthwhile is one of the joys of
living. It can give you a sense of purpose and worth. But you
are more than the sum of your accomplishments. You are
an accomplished woman simply by continuing to mature
into the individual God created you to be. Enjoy using every
gift, talent, and ability God has so generously woven into
you while resting in the fact that you are worthy of God's
love, regardless of what you've achieved.

---

*I'm so thankful for the love and life You've poured
into me. Your blessing and goodness allow me to bless
others with what You've given me. Fill up my heart so
that I may serve You and others with true joy.*

11

Designed for Great Things

Except the LORD build the house,
they labour in vain that build it.

PSALM 127:1

We were designed to do great things hand in hand with a very great God. So why not invite God to be your coworker in every endeavor you undertake today? Call on Him throughout the day, anytime you need wisdom, peace, or perseverance. Allow God to infuse you with creativity, humility, and compassion, regardless of the size of the task at hand. Your hard work, guided by prayer and undergirded by the Spirit of a mighty God, can accomplish amazing things.

My Creator God, Your works are beyond my
understanding and yet You want to partner with me!
I invite You in to do just that. Speak wisdom and
creativity to me as I work today for Your glory.

Self-Image

I will praise thee;
for I am fearfully and wonderfully made.

PSALM 139:14

You are a living, breathing reason for praise. God formed only one of you, unique in appearance, intricate in design, priceless beyond measure. You were fashioned with both love and forethought. When you look in the mirror, is this what you reflect upon? If not, it's time to retrain your brain. Use the mirror as a touchstone to praise. Ask God, "What do You see when You look at me?" Listen quietly as God's truth helps retool your self-image.

Father, please tell me the truth about myself.
Who am I? What do You see? Remind me of the
truth of who I am in Christ. Fill me with Your
radiant love, and let my life praise You.

Discover Beauty

Thy hands have made me and fashioned me: give me
understanding, that I may learn thy commandments.

PSALM 119:73

God isn't concerned with appearances. The Bible tells us
God looks at peoples' hearts instead of what's on the outside.
Perhaps that's because appearances can be deceiving. A
woman can be beautiful in the world's eyes, while her heart
nurtures pride, deceit, lust, greed, or a host of other unlovely
traits. By learning to look at people the way God does, from
the inside out, we may discover beauty in others—and in
ourselves—that we've never noticed before.

Show me what You see when You look at my heart,
Lord. I pray You would fill my insides with the beauty that
comes from knowing You. Help me always
look for that beauty in those around me.

No Greater Assurance

The LORD will perfect that which concerneth me:
thy mercy, O LORD, endureth for ever.

PSALM 138:8

Throughout scripture, God continually reassures us that
He's working on our behalf to accomplish the good things
He has planned for our lives. If your confidence wavers, if
you need to know for certain someone is on your side, if
you're anxious about the future, do what people who've
felt the very same way have done for centuries: Take God's
words to heart. There's no greater assurance than knowing
you're loved, completely and eternally.

Father, I bring all my thoughts and feelings to You at this
moment. Take my worries, and speak truth into my life.
Remind me You are here and at work in my life.

15

Forevermore

The LORD shall preserve thy going out and thy coming in from this time forth, and even for evermore.

PSALM 121:8

Conventional wisdom tells us that nothing lasts forever. Thankfully, just because a saying is often quoted doesn't make it true. The time-tested wisdom of the Bible assures us that God always has been and always will be. Because of Jesus, *forever* is a word that can apply to us as well. When we follow Jesus here on earth, we follow Him straight to heaven. We have the assurance of knowing our true life span is "forevermore."

Jesus, thank You for the amazing truth that eternal life starts here and now. I don't have to wait for heaven to live the abundant life You have for me. May "Your kingdom come" in my life and my actions today.

Attitude Adjustment

*This is the day which the L*ORD* hath made;*
we will rejoice and be glad in it.

PSALM 118:24

What kind of day will you have today? Your answer might be, "I won't know until I've lived it!" But the attitude with which you approach each new day can change the way you experience life. That's why it's important to set aside some "attitude adjustment time" every morning. When you wake, remind yourself, "This is the day the Lord has made." Look for His hand in the details and thank Him for every blessing He brings your way.

I am Yours, and You are mine, Jesus! I go into this day
with this truth at the forefront of my mind.
Have Your way in me, Lord!

Word Pictures

The Lord is my strength and my shield;
my heart trusted in him, and I am helped.

PSALM 28:7

A rock, a fortress, a warrior, a king—the Bible uses many metaphors to describe God. Since no single word can wholly describe our infinite, incomparable God, word pictures help us better connect a God we cannot see with images that we can. If your attitude could use a boost of strength and confidence, picture God as your shield. He is always there to protect you, to shelter you, and to guard your heart and mind.

Creator God, please use the imagination You gave me
to fill me with truths from Your Word. I lay my
thoughts at Your feet for You to transform.

What You Believe

Before the mountains were brought forth,
or ever thou hadst formed the earth and the world,
even from everlasting to everlasting, thou art God.

PSALM 90:2

People once believed the world was flat. This meant only the most intrepid explorers would venture long distances and risk falling off the "edge" of the earth. What people believe determines the choices they make, no matter what era they live in. What do you believe about God? Does it line up with what the Bible says? It's worth checking out. Since you will live what you believe, it's important to be certain that what you believe is true.

Jesus, please speak truth and life into my soul.
I want to follow and believe in the One true God.
Show me any lies I may be believing about You.

Innate Goodness

I had fainted, unless I had believed to see the goodness
of the Lord in the land of the living.

PSALM 27:13

Knowing a friend's heart toward you can help you relax
and be yourself. With a friend like this, you can honestly
share your deepest secrets, feelings, and failures without
fear of ridicule or reprisal. The psalms remind us over and
over again that God's heart toward us is good. Believing in
God's innate goodness means we can entrust every detail
of our lives to Him without hesitation.

Your Word tells me that I am made holy and righteous
because of Christ in me! I am Your beloved
daughter, and You also call me friend.
Thank You for Your great love!

Your Favorite Meal

*But his delight is in the law of the Lord; and in his
law doth he meditate day and night.*

PSALM 1:2

Imagine God's words as your favorite meal, each bite a
delicacy to be savored and enjoyed. You relish the unique
blend of ingredients, the flavor and texture. When the meal
is complete, you're nourished and satisfied. Scripture is a
well-balanced meal for your heart and soul, a meal that can
continue long after your Bible is back on the shelf. Ponder
what you've read. Meditate on God's promises. Chew on
the timeless truths that add zest to your life.

*Jesus, You are my bread of life. You fill me
to overflowing in so many ways.
Thank You for providing for my every need!*

Story of God's Love

Thy testimonies are wonderful:
therefore doth my soul keep them.

PSALM 119:129

The Bible isn't a novel to be read for entertainment, a textbook to be skimmed for knowledge, a manual for living, or a collection of inspirational sayings. The Bible is a love letter. It's the story of God's love for His children from the beginning of the world until the end—and beyond. It's a book that takes time to know well, but God promises His own Spirit will help us understand what we read. All we need to do is ask.

Holy Spirit, I ask You to fill me with love, wisdom,
and understanding as You teach and
convict me from Your Word.

God's Blessings

*Return unto thy rest, O my soul; for the LORD
hath dealt bountifully with thee.*

PSALM 116:7

"Friends know what friends need," so the saying goes.
That's one reason why friends often throw baby showers
for moms-to-be. It's a way to help provide what a mom will
need in the months to come. God knows us, and our needs,
better than any friend or family member does. That's why
He throws us a shower every day. God wraps His blessings
in wisdom, purpose, and creativity to help meet our physical,
emotional, and spiritual needs.

*Father, help me to rest in the truth of who You are.
You are my provider. Help me to stop striving to meet
my own needs and instead let You be Lord of my life.*

Words as Blessings

God be merciful unto us, and bless us;
and cause his face to shine upon us.

PSALM 67:1

When people speak of "blessings," they're often referring to words. Blessings are given at meals and weddings. "Bless you" is even said after a sneeze. The words we say can be as much of a gift as the blessings we can hold in our hands. What would God have you say to the people you meet today? Consider how you can bless others with your words—then speak up. A good word can often be the perfect gift.

Lord, allow me to bless others with my life, my actions,
and my words. I want to bring life and blessing
to people. Show me what that looks like.

Casting Burdens

Cast thy burden upon the LORD,
and he shall sustain thee.

PSALM 55:22

Casting a fishing line is an almost effortless motion. Casting a burden paints a totally different image. Burdens are pictured as heavy, cumbersome, not easily carried—let alone "cast." But casting our burdens on God is as easy as speaking to Him in prayer. It's calling for help when we need it, admitting our sin when we've fallen, and letting our tears speak for our hearts when words fail us.

When my heart is heavy, Lord, You are the only One who
can help. I lay these burdens at Your feet, trusting
that You will carry them for me as I rest in You.

Never Alone

*Blessed be the Lord, who daily loadeth us with
benefits, even the God of our salvation.*

PSALM 68:19

Some things are too heavy to carry alone. A couch, for
instance. Or a washing machine. The same is true for the
mental and emotional burdens we bear. The good news
is that strength, peace, comfort, hope, and a host of other
helping hands are only a prayer away. We're never alone
in our pain or struggle. God is always near, right beside us,
ready to help carry what's weighing us down.

*Lord, You know the heaviness in my heart. Some days
it feels like more than I can bear. Please take these
feelings and issues. Help me to trust that You are bigger.*

Renewed Strength

Great is our Lord, and of great power: his understanding is infinite. The Lord lifteth up the meek.

PSALM 147:5–6

During a track and field event, it isn't uncommon to see an athlete trip over one of the hurdles and tumble to the ground. What brings the crowd to its feet is when the runner gets back up. Challenge involves risk, in sports and in life. Don't be afraid of trying difficult things. Whether you succeed or fail, God promises to renew your strength and purpose. You may not understand how, but you can be certain He's able.

God, I have failed so much in my life. I pray that You would use all of those failures in a way that brings glory to You and draws others to Your heart.

Achieving the Impossible

The LORD is nigh unto all them that call upon him,
to all that call upon him in truth.

PSALM 145:18

Some mornings you wake up with the knowledge that a challenging day is ahead of you. Other times, difficulty catches you by surprise. Whatever challenge enters your life, remind yourself that the Lord is near. Not only will God help you meet each challenge head-on, but He will use each one to help you grow. Look for God's hand at work in your life, helping you achieve what may seem impossible.

My heart is set on You, Lord. Be my eyes and ears
this day. Use each challenge for Your purposes.
Help me to see Your hand in everything.

Perfect, Eternal God

The counsel of the LORD standeth for ever,
the thoughts of his heart to all generations.

PSALM 33:11

Our God isn't wishy-washy. He doesn't experience bad hair days or mood swings, nor is He swayed by trends, fads, or peer pressure. Our perfect, eternal God has no peer. From scripture, we can tell that God experiences emotions like love, grief, and pleasure. However, He isn't driven by His emotions, as we sometimes are. That means we can trust God to be true to His promises, His plans, and His character—today, tomorrow, and always.

Your great love is unfathomable, God! You know all and
still love me lavishly, even when I fail. You see me
as who I am in Christ alone. Thank You, God!

Opportunities

But I trusted in thee, O LORD: I said,
Thou art my God. My times are in thy hand.

PSALM 31:14-15

Change can be exciting. It can also be uncomfortable, unwanted, and at times even terrifying. If you're facing change and find yourself feeling anxious or confused, turn to the God of order and peace. He holds every twist and turn of your life in His hands. Try looking at change through God's eyes, as an opportunity for growth and an invitation to trust Him with your deepest hopes and fears.

Father, please give me spiritual eyes to see things
more like You see them. I want heaven's perspective
on situations and plans. Open my eyes, Lord!

The True You

Examine me, O LORD, and prove me;
try my reins and my heart.

PSALM 26:2

Some women spend a great amount of time trying to look beautiful on the outside, while paying little attention to what's on the inside. God's words and His Spirit can help reveal the true you, from the inside out. Ask God where your character needs some touching up—or perhaps a total makeover. See if your thoughts, your words, and your actions line up with the woman you'd like to see smiling back at you in the mirror each morning.

Search me, Oh God, and know my heart.
Show me anything that is blocking my
relationship with You. Restore me
to Your heart, Lord.

Misunderstood

Let my sentence come forth from thy presence;
let thine eyes behold the things that are equal.

PSALM 17:2

Not everyone will understand the unseen story behind what you say and do. There will be times when you're misunderstood, slandered, or even rejected. This is when your true character shines through. How you respond to adversity and unfair accusations says a lot about you and the God you serve. Ask God to help you address any blind spots you may have about your own character. Treat your critics with respect. Then move ahead with both confidence and humility.

God, it hurts when I'm misunderstood and judged.
I give my heart to You for healing and understanding.
Help me to treat others with respect and grace.

More Than Motherly Love

*That our sons may be as plants grown up in their
youth; that our daughters may be as corner stones,
polished after the similitude of a palace.*

PSALM 144:12

Good food, a good night's sleep, a good education, a good
home that's safe and overflowing with love... Good mothers
try to provide what their children need. But children need
more. Like adults, children have spiritual needs as well
as physical and emotional ones. That's why praying for
your children every day is more than just a good idea. It's
a reminder that your children need more than motherly
love. They also need their heavenly Father's involvement
in their lives.

*Father, I offer up my children to Your loving care.
Help me to care for them and love them well,
but show them where my love comes from.
Reveal Yourself to them individually.*

A Childlike Faith

Lo, children are an heritage of the LORD:
and the fruit of the womb is his reward.

PSALM 127:3

A child is a gift that is literally heaven-sent. You don't have to have children of your own to care about the kids around you—or to learn from them. In the New Testament, Jesus talks about how our faith should resemble that of a child's. To understand why, consider this: Children believe what they hear, love unconditionally, and say what they think. What a wonderful way to relate to God.

Father, breathe new life into my faith. I want to trust
You and enjoy You with the same delight and
wonder that a child has for life.

Wise Choices

*The Lord is the portion of mine inheritance
and of my cup: thou maintainest my lot.*

PSALM 16:5

Some choices we make change the course of our lives, such as whether we'll remain single or marry, what career we'll pursue, whether or not we'll adopt a child. But there's one choice that changes not only the direction of our lives, but also our eternity. When we choose to follow God, it affects every choice we make from that moment forward. The more we involve God in our decision process, the wiser our choices will be.

*God, please fill me with Your life and truth. Let Your Holy
Spirit fill me with wisdom. I take captive each
thought and bring it to You, Jesus.*

Road of Life

*Order my steps in thy word: and let not any
iniquity have dominion over me.*

PSALM 119:133

When you're driving along an unfamiliar highway, road signs are invaluable. They point you in the proper direction and warn you of impending danger. When it comes to the road of life, the Bible is a sign that helps guide you every step of the way. The more you read it, the better prepared you are to make good choices. When facing a fork in the road of life, stop to consider which direction God's Word would have you go.

*As I hide Your Word in my heart, Lord, please use
it to teach me and guide me. Remind me of
Your truths as I make choices each day.*

Perspective and Solace

*The LORD also will be a refuge for the oppressed,
a refuge in times of trouble. And they that know thy
name will put their trust in thee: for thou, LORD,
hast not forsaken them that seek thee.*

PSALM 9:9–10

When women are in need of comfort, they seem to instinctively turn to a spouse or close friend. There's nothing wrong with seeking a human shoulder to cry on when you need it. Just remember that the Bible refers to Jesus as both our bridegroom and friend. The comfort God provides runs deeper than anything people can offer. God sees your problems as part of a larger, eternal picture and can offer perspective as well as solace.

*Jesus, You are my friend and perfect counselor.
Change my desires so that I run to You first before
I go to others. Help me to understand
the reality of who You are.*

Mending a Broken Heart

The LORD is nigh unto them that are of a broken heart;
and saveth such as be of a contrite spirit.

PSALM 34:18

Putting your faith in Jesus doesn't mean you'll never have a broken heart. Scripture tells us even Jesus wept. Jesus knew the future. He knew His heavenly Father was in control. He knew victory was certain. But He still grieved. When your heart is broken, only God has the power to make it whole again. It won't happen overnight. But when you draw close to God, you draw close to the true source of peace, joy, and healing.

You are so close to me when I'm hurting, Father.
Thank You that I don't have to go through this
alone. I offer up all my feelings to You.
Please bring comfort and peace.

God's Commitment

He hath remembered his covenant for ever,
the word which he commanded
to a thousand generations.

PSALM 105:8

God has made a commitment to you similar to a wedding vow. He promises to love and cherish you through sickness and health, prosperity or poverty, good times and bad. But with God, this commitment doesn't last until "death do you part." Even in death and beyond, God is there. There's nothing you can do that will make Him turn His face from you. His commitment to love and forgive you stands steadfast, come what may.

Your Word tells me that nothing—absolutely nothing—not even death can separate me from Your love, Lord. I rest in that truth. My confidence and stability is in You alone.

Consistently Committed

But I will hope continually,
and will yet praise thee more and more.

PSALM 71:14

Choosing to follow God is not a one-time commitment. It's a choice that's made anew each day. Who, or what, will you choose to follow today? Culture or popular opinion? Your emotions or desires? Or God and His Word? Staying consistently committed to anything—a diet, an exercise program, a spouse, or God—takes effort. But with God, His own Spirit strengthens us and gives us hope to help us remain fully committed to Him.

God, please let Your Spirit rise up in me to teach me
and lead me. Show me how to listen for Your
voice in my life. Teach me to do Your will.

Compassion

Like as a father pitieth his children,
so the Lord pitieth them that fear him.

PSALM 103:13

If your children are hurting, you don't think twice about coming to their aid. You listen attentively to their heart-aches, dry their tears, and offer them words of wisdom and encouragement. As God's child, you have a perfect and powerful heavenly Father who feels this way about you. His compassion is more than emotion. It's love in action. You can tell God anything, without fear of condemnation or abandonment. God's forgiveness runs as deep as His love.

God, please restore my heart to see You as a loving
Father. I repent of any thoughts that paint You as
anything but loving and perfect. Because of Jesus,
I stand before You, holy and pleasing in Your sight.

The Heavenly Father's Embrace

*But thou, O Lord, art a God full of
compassion, and gracious, long suffering,
and plenteous in mercy and truth.*

PSALM 86:15

Without love and compassion, an all-powerful God would be something to fear instead of Someone to trust. That's one reason why Jesus came to earth: to help us see the compassionate side of the Almighty. Throughout the Gospels, we read how Jesus reached out to the hurting—the outcasts, the infirm, the poor, and the abandoned. He didn't turn His back on sinners, but embraced them with open arms. His arms are still open. Will you run toward His embrace?

*Thank You, God, for sending Jesus to make a way for me
to approach You in full confidence. You have lifted up
my head and showered me with love and compassion.
Help me to feel Your presence in my life.*

Eternally Confident

My heart is fixed, O God, my heart is fixed:
I will sing and give praise.

PSALM 57:7

In the Bible, when a word or phrase is repeated, it's time to pay attention. In the original language of the Old Testament, this signifies that something is the best, the ultimate, the pièce de résistance! The psalmist in Psalm 57 doubly notes how confident his heart is in God. No wonder praise comes naturally to him! Take it from the psalmist: You need never doubt God's heart toward you. You can be confident—eternally confident—in Him.

Just like the psalmist, I want my heart to be fixed on You,
Lord. Please give me the desire to know You more!
Help me to want the things You want and
to see things the way You see them.

Capable Hands

*Surely he shall not be moved for ever: the righteous shall
be in everlasting remembrance. He shall not be afraid
of evil tidings: his heart is fixed, trusting in the LORD.
His heart is established, he shall not be afraid,
until he see his desire upon his enemies.*

PSALM 112:6-8

We live in uncertain times, economically, politically, and globally. Yet you can greet each new day with your head held high, confident and unafraid. Why? Because you have a God who cares deeply about you and the world around you. When your confidence is placed firmly in God instead of your own abilities, bank account, or "good karma," you need not fear the future. It's in God's powerful, capable, and compassionate hands.

*I put my full trust in You, Lord! All my times are in Your
hands. I've seen You take care of me every day of my life,
and I trust that You will always hold me close.*

True Contentment

The Lord is my shepherd; I shall not want.

PSALM 23:1

When it comes to brains, sheep are not the sharpest crayons in the box. They frighten easily, tend to follow the crowd, and have limited abilities for defending themselves. That's why sheep thrive best with a shepherd who guides, protects, and cares for them. Our Good Shepherd will do the same for us. Worry, fear, and discontent are products of a sheepish mentality. However, the peace of true contentment can be ours when we follow God's lead.

Like sheep who know their master's voice, teach me to hear from You, Lord. I trust You to take care of my needs. Help me to follow You wherever You lead.

Cultivate Contentment

Surely I have behaved and quieted myself,
as a child that is weaned of his mother:
my soul is even as a weaned child.

PSALM 131:2

Picture a well-fed newborn resting in her mother's arms, peacefully gazing up into her eyes. That's contentment. No worrying about "Does this diaper make me look fat?" No fears over "Will social security be around when I retire?" No burning desire for a nicer stroller or a bigger crib. Allow God to baby you. Gaze into His eyes by recalling the ways He's provided for you. Cultivate contentment by trusting Him as a mother is trusted by her child.

Your Word tells me that as a mother comforts her child,
so will You comfort me, Lord. I accept Your comfort.
I want that in my life. Draw me close to You, Father.

Bold and Courageous

In the day when I cried thou answeredst me,
and strengthenedst me with strength in my soul.

Women are often characterized as timid creatures—fleeing from spiders, screaming over mice, cowering behind big, burly men when danger is near. But the Bible characterizes women of God as bold and courageous. Queen Esther risked her life to save God's children from genocide. Deborah led an army and judged the tribes of Israel. Rahab dared to hide Israelite spies to save her family. Today God will supply the courage you need to accomplish whatever He's asked you to do.

Please fill me with boldness and courage that comes
from You alone, heavenly Father. I don't want to be
known for my own strength but for what
You have done through me.

Opportune Time

*Wait on the LORD: be of good courage, and he shall
strengthen thine heart: wait, I say, on the LORD.*

PSALM 27:14

Foolhardiness can look like courage at first glance. However, true courage counts the cost before it forges ahead. If you're faced with a risky decision, it's not only wise to think before you act, it's biblical. Ecclesiastes 3:1 reminds us, "To every thing there is a season, and a time to every purpose under the heaven." Waiting for that right time takes patience and courage. Don't simply pray for courage. Pray for the wisdom to discern that "opportune time."

*Father, I'm asking for wisdom again. I want to sit
in Your presence as You fill me with Your power.
Show me how and when to act on Your promptings.*

Daily Walk

Keep back thy servant also from presumptuous sins;
let them not have dominion over me: then shall
I be upright, and I shall be innocent
from the great transgression.

PSALM 19:13

Yesterday is over. Today is a brand-new day. Any mistakes or bad choices you've made in the past are behind you. God doesn't hold them against you. He's wiped your past clean with the power of forgiveness. The only thing left for you to do with the past is learn from it. Celebrate each new day by giving thanks to God for what He's done and actively anticipating what He's going to do with the clean slate of today.

Father, thank You that Your mercies are new every
morning! I couldn't stand up under the burden
of carrying my past around with me.
Thank You for a brand-new life in Christ!

Relationship

*My voice shalt thou hear in the morning,
O Lord; in the morning will I direct my
prayer unto thee, and will look up.*

PSALM 5:3

Scheduling time to pray and read the Bible can feel like just another item on your to-do list. But getting to know God is not a project. It's a relationship. Best friends don't spend time together just because they feel they should. They do it because they enjoy each other's company and long to know each other better. The more consistent you are in spending time with God each day, the closer of a "friend" you'll feel He is to you.

*Jesus, I'm so amazed that I get to have a personal
relationship with You! Plant a desire in my heart to
seek You and hear from You every day of my life.*

Decisions, Decisions

O my soul, thou hast said unto the LORD,
Thou art my Lord: my goodness extendeth not to thee.

PSALM 16:2

Paper or plastic. Right or left. Yes or no. Every day is filled with decisions that need to be made. Some have little bearing on the big picture of our lives, while others can change its course in dramatic ways. Inviting God into our decision-making process is not only wise, it also helps us find peace with the decisions we make. Knowing God is at work, weaving all our decisions into a life of purpose, helps us move forward with confidence.

I trust Your plan for my life, Lord. I invite You to renew
my mind and transform my thinking. I want my
thoughts and actions to be pleasing to You.

On Track

Good and upright is the LORD:
therefore will he teach sinners in the way.

PSALM 25:8

When you're driving in an unfamiliar city, a map is an invaluable tool. It can help prevent you from taking wrong turns. If you do wind up headed in the wrong direction, a map can help set you back on track. God's Word and His Spirit are like a GPS for your life. Staying in close contact with God through prayer will help you navigate the best route to take in this life, one decision at a time.

Thank You for rerouting me when I take a wrong turn, Father. The end result is always You. When I can't find my way, You gently call me back to Your plans and purposes.

Deepest Longings

Lord, all my desire is before thee;
and my groaning is not hid from thee.

PSALM 38:9

What does your heart long for most? Talk to God about it. He'll help you uncover the true root of your deepest desires. Longing for a child? Perhaps what you're really longing for is unconditional love. Longing for a home of your own? Perhaps it's security or the admiration of others that you crave. Ultimately, God is the only One who can fill your deepest longings—and it's His desire to do exactly that.

Father, I'm asking You to reveal to me the longings of my heart. Show me the truths behind my desires, and shine Your light where I need to see what I'm missing.

God's Delight

Delight thyself also in the LORD: and he shall
give thee the desires of thine heart.

PSALM 37:4

To "delight" in someone is to take great pleasure from simply being in that person's presence. If you truly delight in God, the deepest desire of your heart will be to draw ever closer to Him. This is a desire God Himself delights in filling. That's because God delights in you. You are more than His creation—you are His beloved child. He delights in you like a proud father watching his daughter take her very first steps.

Father please show me the truth of how You see me.
I want to believe that You love me unconditionally,
but sometimes it's just difficult because of my past.
Help me to see myself as Your beloved daughter.

Devotion

And I will walk at liberty: for I seek thy precepts.

PSALM 119:45

Being devoted to someone you love is one thing. Being devoted to doing something, like completing a project or following God's commandments, is quite another. It doesn't sound as passionate or pleasurable, but devoting yourself to do what God asks isn't a self-improvement program. It's a labor of love. Commitment is a way of expressing love, whether it's honoring your marriage vows or devoting yourself to doing what's right. Love is a verb, always in action, making invisible emotions visible.

Your Word tells me that Your burden is light, Lord. When I serve You out of love, You fill my heart with joy and peace. . .not duty! I live my life to praise Your name.

Heart of Devotion

Preserve my soul; for I am holy: O thou my God,
save thy servant that trusteth in thee.

PSALM 86:2

The heart of devotion isn't duty. It's love. The deeper your love, the deeper your devotion. What does being devoted to God look like? It's characterized by a "God first," instead of "me first," mentality. While it's true that being devoted to God means you'll spend time with Him, it also means you'll give your time to others. Your love of God will spill over onto the lives of those around you. Your devotion to God is beneficial to everyone!

Thank You for loving me so well, Lord. I want to follow
You and serve You because You have shown
Your faithfulness and goodness to me.

Answered Prayer

The humble shall see this, and be glad:
and your heart shall live that seek God.

PSALM 69:32

There's encouragement in answered prayer. Sometimes God's answers look exactly like what we were hoping for. Other times they reveal that God's love, wisdom, and creativity far surpass ours. To be aware of God's answers to prayer, we have to keep our eyes and hearts open. Be on the alert for answers to prayer today. When you catch sight of one, thank God. Allow the assurance of God's everlasting care to encourage your soul.

Help me to be aware of Your everyday blessings, Lord.
I want to see Your hand in everything. Open my eyes
and my heart to receive all You have for me.

A Prayer Away

In the day when I cried thou answeredst me,
and strengthenedst me with strength in my soul.

PSALM 138:3

A word of encouragement can go a long way in strengthening our hearts. Whether that word comes from a friend, a spouse, a stranger, or straight from God's own Word, encouragement has power. It lets us know we're not alone. We have a support group cheering us on as we go through life. Out of that support group, God is our biggest fan. He wants us to succeed, and His help is just a prayer away.

Encourage me with Your truth, Lord. Remind me of Your
love and faithfulness. Help me to live each day knowing
the truth about You and who I am in You.

Solid Ground

They that trust in the LORD shall be as mount Zion,
which cannot be removed, but abideth for ever.

PSALM 125:1

Alpine peaks endure sun and showers, heat and hail. They don't yield or bow to adverse conditions, but continue to stand firm, being exactly what God created them to be—majestic mountains. God created you to be a strong, victorious woman. You were designed to endure the changing seasons of this life with God's help. Lean on Him when the winds of life begin to blow. God and His Word are solid ground that will never shift beneath your feet.

When trouble comes, I won't be shaken, because You
hold me firmly in Your hand. I trust You, Lord.
You are my rock and my strong tower.

One Day at a Time

Let my soul live, and it shall praise thee;
and let thy judgments help me.

PSALM 119:175

A marathon runner doesn't start out running twenty-six miles. She has to start slow, remain consistent, and push herself a bit farther day by day. That's how endurance is built. The same is true in life. If what lies ahead seems overwhelming, don't panic or think you need to tackle everything at once. Ask God to help you do what you can today. Then celebrate the progress you've made, rest, and repeat. Endurance only grows one day at a time.

Forgive me for my worries, Lord. Help me to stay in the
present moment. . .with You. When I'm overwhelmed,
lead me to the rock that is higher than I.

Eternal Life

*Every day will I bless thee; and I will praise
thy name for ever and ever.*

PSALM 145:2

Eternal life isn't a reward we can earn. It's a free gift given
by a Father who wants to spend eternity with the children
He loves. This gift may be free to us, but it was purchased
at a high price. Jesus purchased our lives at the cost of
His own. His death on the cross is the bridge that leads us
from this life into the next. Forever isn't long enough to
say thank you for a gift like that.

*Jesus, help me to never take Your great sacrifice for
granted. I'm free because You paid dearly for my
freedom. Let me live my life in thanksgiving.*

Childlike Wonder

*Thou wilt shew me the path of life: in thy presence
is fulness of joy; at thy right hand there
are pleasures for evermore.*

PSALM 16:11

Johann Wolfgang von Goethe wrote, "Life is the childhood of our immortality." In light of eternity, you're just a kid—regardless of your age. In today's youth-obsessed society, keeping your "true" age in mind can help you see each day from a more heavenly perspective. Hold on to your sense of childlike wonder. Allow it to inspire awe, thanks, praise, and delight. Draw near to your heavenly Father and celebrate. There's so much more to your life than meets the eye.

*Father, I ask that You give me a heavenly perspective
on this world. . .and on my life. I want to live with the
faith of a child, in awe of who You are and
what You have in store for me.*

Ultimate Example

I will meditate in thy precepts,
and have respect unto thy ways.
PSALM 119:15

In the Bible we read about heroes like Abraham, Moses, and David. Though these men did admirable things, they were also flawed. They made mistakes and poor choices. Nevertheless, God used them in remarkable ways. The only person in the Bible who lived a perfect life was Jesus. He is our ultimate example. If you're searching for the best way to live and love, Jesus' footsteps are the only ones wholly worth following.

Thank You for using me despite my flaws, Lord.
I bring them all to You to create whatever You
would make of my life. My life is Yours, God.

An Example Worth Following

I am as a wonder unto many;
but thou art my strong refuge.

PSALM 71:7

If people follow your example, where will it lead? Will they find themselves headed toward God or away from Him? As you allow God to change you from the inside out, your life will naturally point others in His direction. Being an example worth following doesn't mean you're under pressure to be perfect. It's God's power shining through the lives of imperfect people that whispers most eloquently, "There's more going on here than meets the eye. God is at work."

God, I ask You to take a look in my heart and examine me.
I want You to change me from the inside out so
that my life points others to You.

Expect Great Things

*Be of good courage, and he shall strengthen
your heart, all ye that hope in the LORD.*

PSALM 31:24

Trusting God can help transform you into a "glass half full" kind of person. You can face every day, even the tough ones, with confidence and expectation because you're aware there's more to this life than can be seen. You can rest in the promise that God is working all things together for your good. You know death is not the end. In other words, you can expect that great things lie ahead. Why not anticipate them with thanks and praise?

*I praise You, Lord, for who You are and for Your great
plans for me. I trust You to work out all things
for my good and for Your glory.*

Praying in Expectation

The eyes of all wait upon thee; and thou givest
them their meat in due season.

PSALM 145:15

Praying without expecting God to answer is kind of like
wishing on a star. You don't believe it's going to make any
difference, but you do it anyway—just in case there really
is something behind all those fairy tales. When you pray,
do so with great expectations. God is at work on behalf of a
child He dearly loves—you. Just remember, God's answers
may arrive in ways and at a time that you least expect.

Your Word tells me that prayer is powerful and effective.
I trust in You, Lord. I trust that You have my best
interests at heart as You answer my prayers.

The Better You Know God

The LORD preserveth the simple:
I was brought low, and he helped me.

PSALM 116:6

Feel like you need more faith? Sometimes what we really need is the courage to act on what we already believe. A skydiver may have faith her parachute is packed correctly, but that doesn't stop her stomach from doing its own loop-de-loop as she jumps out of the plane. However, the more she dives, the less nervous she feels. The better you know God, the more a leap of faith feels like a hop into a loving Father's waiting arms.

Just as the man talking to Jesus said "Lord, I believe,
help thou mine unbelief," I want to believe more too,
Lord. Fill me with a desire to know You more.

Gift of Faith

*Lead me in thy truth, and teach me: for thou art the God
of my salvation; on thee do I wait all the day.*

PSALM 25:5

Faith is both a gift we receive and an action we take. God's
Spirit gives us enough faith to reach out to a Father we
cannot see. But as we continue reaching—continue putting
our trust in God as we go through life—that little gift of faith
grows stronger, like a muscle consistently put to work at
the gym. Give your faith a workout today by doing what
you believe God wants you to do.

*Help me to live by faith and not by sight, Lord. You've
already provided all the evidence I need. I look at the
world and people around me, and I see Your handiwork.*

Unshakable

For the LORD is good; his mercy is everlasting;
and his truth endureth to all generations.

PSALM 100:5

With time, we come to believe certain things are unshakable. The sun rises and sets. The tides ebb and flow. Seasons revolve year after year. Babies are born, people die, and the world goes on pretty much as it has for centuries: faithful to a predictable pattern. But there will come a time when the world as we know it will end. Only God is totally unshakable and unchanging. His love and goodness to us will remain forever faithful.

Lord, You are good to me, and I trust Your promises.
I give You any doubts and fears about my future,
and I trust Your heart for Your people.

Promises Kept

Thy kingdom is an everlasting kingdom,
and thy dominion endureth throughout
all generations.

PSALM 145:13

There's an old saying that warns, "Promises are made to be broken." With God, the opposite is true. The Bible is filled with promises God has made and kept. With a track record like that, it means you can trust God's Word and His love for you. He remains faithful, even if your faithfulness to Him wavers from time to time. God and His promises have stood the test of time and will remain steadfast throughout eternity.

You are always faithful to me, Lord. You are
the perfect parent, and Your love for me
never wavers. I trust You with my life.

Unconditional Love

God setteth the solitary in families.

PSALM 68:6

Family can be one of our greatest joys in this life. It can also be messy, because it's where we show our true colors. It's where we're real. That's why "family" is the perfect petri dish for us to learn how to love like Jesus. Unconditional love sees others for who they really are, warts and all, and continues to reach out, sacrifice, and forgive. As we allow God to love us, He will help us more readily love others.

Lord, I cannot truly love others without Your Spirit at work in me. Show me how to love like You do. Infuse me with Your power so I can do it.

True Lineage

For thou, O God, hast heard my vows:
thou hast given me the heritage of
those that fear thy name.

PSALM 61:5

Your true lineage extends far beyond the branches on your family tree. That's because you have a spiritual heritage as well as a physical one. Your family line extends back through Old and New Testament times, around the world, and right up into today. You may know some of your brothers and sisters by name. Others you may not meet until you walk the streets of heaven together. But God's children are family, linked by faith and a forever future.

Thank You for the family of God You have given me,
Father. Please continue to bring people into
my life who help draw me closer to You.

More Than a Passing Acquaintance

They looked unto him, and were lightened:
and their faces were not ashamed.

PSALM 34:5

People often ask "How are you?" as a formality. What they want to hear is "Fine!" Nothing more. But God wants more than a passing acquaintance with you. He invites you to share not only what you want and need, but also how you feel. God created you as a woman with complex emotions. You need never hesitate to share your tears, or even a hormonal outburst, with the One who knows you and loves you through and through.

Creator God, You made me beautifully feminine,
and I accept that and join You in Your will for me as
a woman. I ask Your blessing on my life as I seek You.

What Is Real

In the multitude of my thoughts
within me thy comforts delight my soul.

PSALM 94:19

What are your emotions telling you today? You're unloved? Insignificant? A failure? Powerless to change? What you feel is not always an accurate measure of what is real. When your emotions try to take you on a roller-coaster ride, refuse to buckle yourself in. Ask God to help you sort through what's going on in your mind and heart. Cling to what God says is true, not to what your fickle emotions whisper on a poor self-image day.

Remind me of who I am in Christ, Father. You see me
as holy, clothed with the righteousness of
Christ. I can do all things through You.

Experiencing Fellowship

*I will praise thee for ever, because thou hast done it: and I
will wait on thy name; for it is good before thy saints.*

PSALM 52:9

Fellowship is a fancy word for getting together with others
who love God. It's more than going to church. It's doing
life together. Whether you're meeting as a small group
for Bible study or simply chatting one-on-one over a cup
of coffee about what God is doing in your lives, you're
experiencing fellowship. When faith and friendship come
together with honesty and authenticity, relationships
thrive—between you and God and between you and your
spiritual brothers and sisters.

*Father, please place God-honoring people in my life
who speak the truth in loving ways. Fill us with
joy as we gather together in Your presence.*

God's Church

I will give thee thanks in the great congregation:
I will praise thee among much people.

PSALM 35:18

There's beauty and power in drawing close to God each morning to talk to Him about the day ahead. But you are just one of God's children. Sometimes it's great to get the family together for prayer and worship. Every Sunday, in churches around the world, that's exactly what's happening. God's family is getting together for a Thanksgiving celebration. Like any family get-together, your presence adds to the joy. So join in! God's church wouldn't be the same without you.

Thank You for making me a part of the body of Christ.
What an amazing honor to be called Your daughter!
I join my family in praising You, heavenly Father.

True Value

Trust not in oppression, and become not vain in robbery:
if riches increase, set not your heart upon them.

PSALM 62:10

Money is an important tool. You can use it to repair your car, pay your rent, or help put food on the table. But it's just a tool. Loving it would be like loving a socket wrench. It can't love you back or change who you are. It can only do its job. Ultimately, the true value of a tool depends on how well you use it. Allow God to show you how to wield your finances wisely.

Thank You for Your many blessings, Father. My finances
are Yours. Train me to be thankful and to use them
wisely to care for the needs of those around me.

Increase in Value

Be not thou afraid when one is made rich,
when the glory of his house is increased.

PSALM 49:16

It's been said that "money talks." Sometimes it yells. Loudly. The things it buys help draw attention to those who have it and to those who would do anything to get it. But money says absolutely nothing about who a person really is—or how rich he or she truly is. You have riches that exceed what's in your bank account. Every relationship you invest in, be it with God, family, or friends, is a treasure that increases in value over time.

Father, thank You for teaching me that my value
has nothing to do with the money I make. I am
valuable simply because I'm Your child.

Perfectly Forgiving

For thou, Lord, art good, and ready to forgive;
and plenteous in mercy unto all them
that call upon thee.

PSALM 86:5

The fact that God is perfect can be intimidating, especially when you consider that God knows everything you've ever done. But our perfect God is also perfectly forgiving. There is nothing you can do, or have done, that will make Him turn away from you. When you ask for forgiveness, you have it. No groveling. No begging. All you need to do is come to Him in humility and truth. Jesus has taken care of the rest.

I'm so amazed at Your great love for me, Lord God!
You can never love me more or less than You do right
now. Thank You for Your grace and love in my life.

An Empty Chalkboard

As far as the east is from the west, so far hath
he removed our transgressions from us.

PSALM 103:12

Picture a chalkboard. Written on it is everything you've ever done that goes against what God has asked of you. What would you see written there? How big would the chalkboard be? Now imagine God wiping it clean with one swipe of His hand. Nothing remains, not the faintest image of one single word. That's how completely God has forgiven you. When guilt or shame over past mistakes threatens to creep back into your life, remember the empty chalkboard—and rejoice.

I cannot praise You enough for cleaning my slate,
Lord Jesus. The truth of who You are and
what You've done are astonishing to me.
I put my whole heart in Your hands.

Without Condition

And my soul shall be joyful in the LORD:
it shall rejoice in his salvation.

PSALM 35:9

Knowing you're loved without condition sets you free. It invites you to abandon insecurity, relax, and enjoy being yourself. It encourages you to go ahead and try, because failure is simply a steep learning curve. God's acceptance of you is the key to this freedom. As you rest in God's absolute acceptance, you'll discover the confidence and courage you need to push beyond who you are today and become the woman you were created to be.

Lord, help me to live my life knowing You are pleased
with me. . .instead of trying to please others and following
the social rules of the day. Help me to enjoy just
being who You created me to be.

Rules

I will run the way of thy commandments,
when thou shalt enlarge my heart.

PSALM 119:32

Suppose there were no traffic laws. Going out for a drive would be a dangerous endeavor. Drivers would have to fight their way down the road. Traffic would be a snarled mess. Following rules can sound like the opposite of freedom. But without rules, community turns into chaos. Following God's commands protects us from harm and helps us love God and others well. It frees us to travel the road of life unencumbered by fear, uncertainty, or insecurity.

Please place a desire for healthy boundaries
in my life, Lord. Show me what that looks
like so I can follow You in confidence.

Friendship

But to the saints that are in the earth,
and to the excellent, in whom is all my delight.

PSALM 16:3

Thank God for friendship. Literally. Spending time with those who understand how you tick, remind you what a wonderful woman you are, and challenge you to reach your God-given potential is one of life's greatest joys. The best way to have great friends is to be one. Pray regularly for the women God brings into your life, asking God to help you love them in ways that help you grow closer to each other and to Him.

Thank You for my friends, Lord. Draw our hearts closer
to You and to each other, as we encourage one
another in our faith. Help us to love well.

Smoothing Rough Edges

Behold, how good and how pleasant it is for
brethren to dwell together in unity!

PSALM 133:1

The feel of sandpaper rubbing against unfinished wood isn't pleasant. Neither is the experience of two good friends rubbing each other the wrong way. But when friends are authentic and vulnerable with each other, it's bound to happen—and that's a good thing. It helps bring our weaknesses to light. Helping smooth out one another's rough edges is part of God's plan. If friendship hits a rough patch, stay close and work through the friction. Let love help you grow.

Lord, please allow my friends and me to sharpen one
another. Let love guide all of our thoughts and
actions toward each other as we show
grace and truth in our friendships.

Seeds

Thy wife shall be as a fruitful vine by the sides of thine house: thy children like olive plants round about thy table.

PSALM 128:3

There are many ways to be fruitful. One way is through relationships. Whether it's with family, friends, neighbors, church members, or coworkers, the things you say and do can be buds that blossom into something beautiful. Who will you spend time with today? Each encounter is an opportunity to plant a seed. Will it be a seed of encouragement, grace, faith, comfort, or. . . ? Ask God to help you know the type of seed others need.

Father, please bring people into my life who need encouragement from me. I also ask that You would put me on the path of those who can encourage me as well. Help me to know what seeds need to be sown.

The Harvest

And let the beauty of the LORD our God be upon us:
and establish thou the work of our hands upon us;
yea, the work of our hands establish thou it.

PSALM 90:17

If you plant an apple tree, you probably hope to enjoy its fruit someday. But hoping, and even praying, won't guarantee a good harvest. A fruit tree needs to be watered, pruned, and protected from bugs, frost, and hail. It needs God's gift of life and your loving care. The same is true for any project you're working on. Work hard, pray hard, and wait patiently for God's good timing. Then, when harvesttime arrives, remember to give thanks.

Please give me eyes to see Your hands at work all around me, Creator God. I want to be in on the work You are doing in my little portion of the world.

"Happy Eternally After"

Thine eyes did see my substance, yet being unperfect;
and in thy book all my members were written,
which in continuance were fashioned,
when as yet there was none of them.

PSALM 139:16

The story of your life is written one day at a time. Every choice you make influences the chapters yet to come. But one thing is certain—the ending. Your future was written the moment you chose to follow God. That means the end of your story here on earth is actually a brand-new beginning. It's a story with endless chapters, a "happy eternally after" where tears are history and true love never fails.

I trust You as I journey on this earth, Lord. I don't know
all the future holds, but I do know that You hold my
future. I trust Your unfailing love for me!

God Is at Work

The lines are fallen unto me in pleasant places;
yea, I have a goodly heritage.

PSALM 16:6

It's been said that we don't know what the future holds, but we know who holds the future. Tomorrow is not a potluck of chance possibilities. The Bible tells us that God is at work, bringing something good out of every situation His children face. Knowing a God who deeply loves us and is in control, no matter what comes our way, allows us to hold our heads high and walk toward the future with confident expectation.

My only hope is in You, Lord. My confidence is in You.
My faith is in You. I am so thankful that
I can trust You with my life.

Grateful Generosity

A good man sheweth favour, and lendeth:
he will guide his affairs with discretion.

PSALM 112:5

A funny thing happens when you get in the habit of sharing what God has given you. The more you give, the more you realize how blessed you are and the more grateful you become—which inspires you to share even more of what you have with others. It's a wonderful cycle that loosens your grip on material things so both your hands and your heart can more freely reach out to those around you.

I offer up everything I have to You, Lord. It all belongs
to You anyway. Lead me to bless others with what You
have given me. Help me to show love in tangible ways.

Loving Generosity

The wicked borroweth, and payeth not again:
but the righteous sheweth mercy, and giveth.

PSALM 37:21

Love and generosity are two sides of the same coin. Both put the needs of others before their own. Both give without expecting anything in return. Both make our invisible God more visible to a world in need. As our love for those around us grows, generosity can't help but follow suit. Today, take time to become more aware of the needs of those around you. Then ask God to help you act on what you see with loving generosity.

Lord, every time I have given unselfishly, You pour more
blessings back into my life. The greatest blessing
of all is Your presence in my life.

God's Gentleness

Teach me to do thy will; for thou art my God:
thy spirit is good; lead me into the land of uprightness.

PSALM 143:10

God doesn't drag His children through life by the wrist like a domineering parent with a self-centered agenda. God leads with love, gently and quietly. God's Spirit whispers, "Go this way," as a verse of scripture crosses your mind. He tenderly nudges your conscience toward making good choices and reaching out in love. He brings comfort in countless creative ways that those who don't recognize Him label as coincidence. God's gentleness reminds us that His power is always tempered by love.

Your Word tells us that we can hear and know Your voice, Lord. Quiet my mind to hear Your voice more clearly. I want to follow You.

Closer. . .

Thou hast also given me the shield of thy salvation:
and thy right hand hath holden me up,
and thy gentleness hath made me great.

PSALM 18:35

A children's fable describes the sun and wind making a bet: Who can get a man to take off his coat? The wind blows with vengeance, using his strength to try and force the man's hand. The sun simply shines, gently inviting the man to shed what he no longer needs. God does the same with us. His gentleness warms us toward love and faith. The closer we draw to God, the more we'll treat others as He's treated us.

Father, fill me with Your love and gentleness.
Change my motives and actions to match the
fruit of Your Spirit. Draw me closer to Your heart.

God's Goodness

O fear the LORD, ye his saints:
for there is no want to them that fear him.

PSALM 34:9

In the Old Testament book of Exodus, we read about Moses, a man God referred to as "friend." When Moses asks to see God's glory, God shows Moses His goodness. Afterward, Moses' face literally glows. When we worship God, we glimpse His goodness. We focus on who He is, what He's done, and what He's promised is yet to come. Our faces may not glow like Moses', but glimpsing God's goodness is bound to bathe our hearts in joy.

Your Word tells me that those who look to You are radiant; their faces are never covered in shame. Thank You for filling me with Your Spirit, Lord God!

Something Good

*O my soul, thou hast said unto the LORD, Thou art my
Lord: my goodness extendeth not to thee.*

PSALM 16:2

What is good about your life? Consider how every good
thing we receive can be traced back to God. Family. Friends.
Talents. The ability to earn an income. It's easy to take the
good things in our lives for granted, while readily putting
the blame on God when we feel things go wrong. The next
time you notice you're feeling happy about something
good in your life, look for the part God played in sending
it your way.

*You are so good to me, Lord! You fill my life with good
things. I see Your hand in everything I have.
Thank You for the life You've given me.*

Wrapped in Grace

*For the LORD God is a sun and shield: the LORD
will give grace and glory: no good thing will he
withhold from them that walk uprightly.*

PSALM 84:11

When a gift is wrapped in grace, it comes with no strings attached. That's the kind of gift God gives. He doesn't hold eternal life just out of reach, taunting, "If you try harder, this can be yours." He doesn't promise to love us if we never mess up again. He doesn't say He'll forgive, but refuse to forget. God graces us with gifts we don't deserve, because His love is deeper than our hearts and minds can comprehend.

*I cannot comprehend the depths of Your grace and love,
Lord. I trust that You do not hold my past against me.
Your forgiveness is eternal. Thank You for
wrapping me in grace.*

Grateful Acceptance

The LORD is good to all: and his tender
mercies are over all his works.

If a driver in front of you unexpectedly pays your toll, you
can't help but feel in her debt. It's a kindness you didn't
deserve and can't repay. Jesus' death on the cross was more
than a random act of kindness. It was part of an eternal
plan. It was also a gift of grace. Jesus paid a high toll for
your sins. You can't repay Him. All you can do is gratefully
accept what He's given.

You draw me to You by Your lovingkindness,
heavenly Father. I accept who You are and
what You've done for me. I can't repay You,
but I can live in a place of thankfulness.

Vantage Point

*I will instruct thee and teach thee in the way which
thou shalt go: I will guide thee with mine eye.*

PSALM 32:8

If you're on a safari, a knowledgeable guide will lead you
to the best vantage point to see wildlife, educate you on
what you're seeing, and protect you from danger. God is
like a safari guide who never leaves your side. He knows
both the joys and the dangers that surround you. Through
His Spirit and scripture, God will guide you toward a life
of wonder and adventure. Stay close to His side and allow
Him to lead.

*I accept You as my heavenly guide, Holy Spirit.
I want more of You in my life. You are my counselor
and my teacher. I commit to follow where You lead.*

Better Acquainted

I will bless the LORD, who hath given me counsel:
my reins also instruct me in the night seasons.

PSALM 16:7

Suppose you learn CPR in a first-aid class. Years later, when a child nearly drowns at a neighborhood pool, you spring into action. You know exactly what to do. The same is true with the Bible. The better acquainted you become with God's words, the more readily they come to mind when you need them most. When you're unsure of which way to turn, turn to the Bible. It will help lead you where you ultimately want to go.

Father, please give me a deep desire for
Your Word. I want to spend time with You,
learning Your truth and knowing You more.

Glimpses of God

*Glory ye in his holy name: let the heart of them rejoice
that seek the L ORD . Seek the L ORD , and his
strength: seek his face evermore.*

P SALM 105:3-4

Babies often smile when they catch sight of their mother's
face. Catching a glimpse of God can do the same for us.
It can make our hearts happy. Yet God's presence is much
more subtle than that of a human parent. God reveals
Himself in quiet ways, such as in an answer to prayer, the
glory of a sunset, or the gift of a new friend. Keep your eyes
open. God is ever present and at work in your life.

*Father, I want to see You at work in my life. Open my
spiritual eyes to see You. Thank You in advance
for answering my prayers in this way.*

Nurturing a Happy Heart

*Because thou hast been my help, therefore in the
shadow of thy wings will I rejoice.*

PSALM 63:7

Happiness can be contagious. Why not spread some of
yours around? Consider the ways God helps you nurture a
happy heart. How has He comforted you, encouraged you,
strengthened you? If you're happy, share it. Tell someone
close to you what God has done. Smile warmly at those who
cross your path. Surprise someone with a gift just because.
Express to God how you feel in song. Thank God for the
little things—such as the ability to feel happy.

*Father, will You fill my heart with contagious joy?
I want to spread Your love to those who need it most.
Help me to show deep, authentic love to those around me.*

Hope and Healing

My flesh and my heart faileth: but God is the strength
of my heart, and my portion for ever.

PSALM 73:26

Your body is amazingly resilient, yet terminally fragile. Fashioned by God's lovingly creative hand, it was not designed to last. But you were. That's because you are so much more than your body. But God cares about all of you, your body and your soul. Even if your health fails, He will not. He is near. He hears every prayer, even those you hesitate to pray. Call on Him. His hope and healing reach beyond this life into the next.

Your Word tells me that You set eternity in my heart when You created me, Lord. Thank You for loving me that much! I can't wait to be with You for all eternity.

Healthy Habits

He healeth the broken in heart,
and bindeth up their wounds.

PSALM 147:3

Good health is a matter of both prayer and practice. As with every detail of our lives, God wants us to share our health concerns with Him. But God also asks us to take an active role in caring for our bodies. The way we care for a gift reveals what we truly feel about the giver, as well as what we've received. Practicing healthy habits is a thank-you note to God for His gift of life.

Father, I pray that You would give me wisdom
to seek healthy habits in my mind, body, and spirit.
I am Your temple. Help me to treat my
body in a way that honors You.

The Impossible

Arise, O Lord; O God, lift up thine hand:
forget not the humble.

PSALM 10:12

God spoke the cosmos into being. He fashioned the ebb and flow of the tides. He breathed life into what was once nothing more than dust. This same awesome God is reaching down to offer His help to you today. Perhaps your prayer is for your own needs. Or maybe it's for those you care about but don't know how to help. God is mighty enough, and loving enough, to do the impossible.

Lord, I believe You can do more than all I could ask
or imagine! I trust that You are the Creator of all,
and that You want an intimate relationship with me.

Every Prayer

LORD, *thou hast heard the desire of the humble:*
thou wilt prepare their heart, thou wilt
cause thine ear to hear.

PSALM 10:17

Help! is a prayer every heart knows how to pray, even those who are unsure if there's a God who's listening. It's a cry that acknowledges that life is out of our control—and a deep-seated hope that Someone is ultimately in charge. Our desperate cries do not disappear into thin air. God hears every prayer, sees every tear, and doesn't hesitate to act. God's answers and timing are not always what we expect, but they are what we need.

What an amazing thought. . . You actually care about
and count my tears, Lord! I'm so grateful that You
are near and that You care. I love You, Lord!

No Secrets

Commit thy way unto the LORD; trust also in him;
and he shall bring it to pass.

PSALM 37:5

You can't keep a secret from God. He knows you inside and out. That doesn't mean you can't hold out on Him. There may be things you'd rather not discuss: areas of shame, bitterness, or rebellion. He'll never muscle His way into those parts of your heart. He's waiting for an invitation. If you're honest about wanting real change in your life, don't wait any longer. Open up before God. Grace, forgiveness, and healing are yours for the asking.

You are so gentle and loving with me, God.
Thank You for Your lovingkindness. I want to
open my whole heart to You. Show me the way.

Living the Truth

Mark the perfect man, and behold the upright:
for the end of that man is peace.

PSALM 37:37

Honesty is more than just telling the truth. It's living it. When you conform to the expectations of those around you instead of focusing on maturing into the individual God designed you to be, you rob the world of something priceless—the unique gift of you. You also rob yourself of the joy and freedom that come from fulfilling your God-given potential. When it comes to being the true you, honesty truly is the best policy.

Help me to bless my personality instead of curse it
by trying so hard to conform to the personalities of
others. Help me to live out exactly who
You made me to be, Father.

Hope

Happy is he that hath the God of Jacob for his help,
*whose hope is in the L*ORD *his God.*

PSALM 146:5

Some people place their hope in financial security. Others hope their popularity, abilities, or connections will get them where they want to go. Still others hope that if they want something badly enough, it'll just happen. But only those who place their hope in God can face tomorrow without any fear of the future. When you trust in God, you do more than hope for the best. You rest in knowing God's best is His plan for your life.

My only hope is in You, Lord. Please make that the desire
and the truth of my life. Forgive me for the times
I hope in my own plans instead of Yours.

Reconnect

The LORD is nigh unto them that are of a broken heart;
and saveth such as be of a contrite spirit.

PSALM 34:18

It's easy to lose heart when your focus is on difficulties that persist day after day. That's why reconnecting with God every morning is so important. Time together reminds you that an all-knowing and all-powerful God is in your corner, ready and able to help. It helps you sift the trivial from the eternal. And it restores hope to its rightful place in your life, where it can shine a light on God's goodness and faithfulness to you.

When I'm broken, I praise You that You come close
to me. I trust that You are near and that You
will comfort me in every pain and difficulty.

True Humility

Though the LORD be high, yet hath he respect unto
the lowly: but the proud he knoweth afar off.

PSALM 138:6

Beloved child, rebellious daughter; faithful friend, self-centered competitor; fully forgiven, fickle and flawed; priceless miracle, nothing but dust: You are the sum of all of these things and more. Acknowledging that you're a crazy quilt of weakness and strength is a step toward humility. After all, true humility isn't regarding yourself as less significant than others. It's seeing yourself the way God does, as no more or less than you truly are.

Father, help me see myself the way You see me.
Knowing that I have done nothing to deserve the
amazing gift of Christ's righteousness...
yet You love me still. Amazing!

Steering Wheel

*And in thy majesty ride prosperously because of
truth and meekness and righteousness; and thy
right hand shall teach thee terrible things.*

PSALM 45:4

Remembering that only God is God keeps us humble.
Sounds simple enough. But all too often we try to grab the
wheel from God's hands and steer our lives in the direction
of what looks like it will make us happy instead of simply
doing what God asks us to do. Invite God to expose any
areas of your life where pride has you heading in the wrong
direction. Ask Him to reveal to you how big He really is.

*Lord, help me to be still and know that You alone are
God. Show me how big and all-powerful You are. . .
and at the same time so intimate and loving.*

Full Life

Blessed are the undefiled in the way,
who walk in the law of the LORD.

PSALM 119:1

Modern culture tells us that "bad girls" have all the fun. Don't believe it. A self-centered life is an empty life. When you choose to follow God and live a life of integrity, regret no longer knocks at your door. In its place, you find joy. There are no worries about your past catching up with you or some half-truth being exposed. You're ready to live life to the fullest, a life in which love and respect are freely given and received.

Life with You, Lord, is a great adventure! Remind me of
that every day. No day is boring when I have my
heart set on You and Your plans for me.

Consistency

I will behave myself wisely in a perfect way.
O when wilt thou come unto me? I will walk
within my house with a perfect heart.

PSALM 101:2

Chameleons may be interesting to watch on the nature channel, but they're not something worth emulating in terms of character. Consistency in the way we live our lives—whether we're on the job, at home with family, or out on the town with friends—is a hallmark of integrity. If how we act is dependent on who we're with, we may be seeking the approval of others more than seeking God. In terms of integrity, whose approval are you seeking today?

Lord, help me to always be true to You and to myself.
I want to look in the mirror each day knowing that
I'm honoring You in all my words and deeds.

At Home in Your Heart

They also that dwell in the uttermost parts are afraid
at thy tokens: thou makest the outgoings of
the morning and evening to rejoice.

PSALM 65:8

Happiness is usually the result of circumstance. Joy, how-ever, bubbles up unbidden, often persisting in spite of circumstance. It's an excitement that simmers below the surface, an assurance that God is working behind the scenes, a contentment that deepens as you discover your place in the world. The more at home you feel with God, the more joy will make a home in your heart—a welcome reminder that God is near.

Fill me with joy as I continue to seek Your presence,
heavenly Father. I want to understand and exhibit joy
in my relationships, reminding everyone
that You are near.

Into the Light

*Thou hast turned for me my mourning into
dancing: thou hast put off my sackcloth,
and girded me with gladness.*

PSALM 30:11

Some seasons of life pull you into the shadows. But God
wants to help you make your way back into the light—not
because you shouldn't mourn, but because every season
heralds a new beginning. There is joy ahead, even if you
can't see it or feel it right now. Each day brings you closer
to those first flutters of joy. Watch for them. Wait for them.
Pray for them. Then celebrate their arrival with thanks
and praise.

*Father, I ask that You fill my heart and my home with joy!
Let the season of joy return to my family. Thank You
for pouring the fruits of Your Spirit into my heart.*

Justice

The mouth of the righteous speaketh wisdom,
and his tongue talketh of judgment.

PSALM 37:30

It takes courage to stand up for what's right, especially if
you're the only voice speaking up in the crowd. But words
have power. They can help bring injustice to light. They can
encourage others to take a stand. They can incite change.
But the right motive is just as important as the right words.
Ephesians 4:15 tells us to speak "the truth in love." Truth
tempered with love is the perfect agent of change.

Lord, help me to stand up for justice.
Give me courage and boldness to speak—
and the wisdom to know when the time is right.

In His Perfect Time

*The LORD executeth righteousness
and judgment for all that are oppressed.*

PSALM 103:6

If watching the evening news leaves you feeling that life isn't fair, take it as a sign that you've inherited your heavenly Father's sense of justice. The way people are treated in this world is not always fair or loving. Sometimes they're used, abused, and then tossed aside. But with God, justice will prevail. God knows each person's story and will make things right in His perfect time and in His wise and loving ways.

*I can hardly wait for the day when our stories will be
told from Your perspective, Lord. You see the truth,
and I wait patiently for You to make things right.*

Others' Hearts

Kindness turns criticism into encouragement, bad news into words of comfort, and discipline into teachable moments. That's because kindness is concerned with more than results. It's also concerned with people's hearts. God's plan for you is bigger than being a "good person." God also wants you to be healed and whole. You can trust God to be a loving Father and not a callous taskmaster, because the breadth of His kindness stems from the depth of His love.

Father, I praise You that You came to heal my heart
and set me free! Your kindness is unwavering.
Pour Your kindness into me so I can in
turn pour kindness into others.

Quiet Side of Love

Bless the LORD, O my soul,
and forget not all his benefits.

PSALM 103:2

Kindness is a quiet side of love. It isn't showy, demanding center stage. It often serves in the background, meeting needs, offering a word of encouragement or an impromptu hug. Sometimes kindness even travels under the name "anonymous." Likewise, the kindnesses God showers upon our lives often fall into the anonymous category. They're the coincidences, the unexpected pleasures, the little things that lift our hearts during a difficult day. How has God's kindness enriched your life this week?

Help me to see that as my fellow believers, the "body of Christ," show kindness to me. . .it is really You showering me with Your loving-kindness. I praise Your name!

Leadership

*Thou leddest thy people like a flock
by the hand of Moses and Aaron.*

PSALM 77:20

Think of the leaders in your life. The list may include a boss, pastor, Bible study leader, mentor, chairperson, or the government officials helping to steer the direction of the country you live in. The Bible encourages us to support and pray for our leaders. It doesn't add a disclaimer, saying this applies only if we like them, agree with them, or voted for them. How would God have you pray for your leaders today?

*Lord, I lift up the leaders in my life to You. From my
local church body to the leaders of my country,
I ask Your will to be done in their lives.*

Following Footsteps

Put not your trust in princes, nor in the son of man,
in whom there is no help.

PSALM 146:3

Those we choose to follow have power over us. Their influence can affect our actions, as well as our way of thinking. They can help draw us closer to or steer us further away from God. But sometimes we're not even aware of whom we're letting lead. Celebrities, experts in various fields, the media, charismatic friends—whose footsteps are you following? Ask God to help you discern who besides Him is worthy to lead the way for you.

Father, forgive me for putting my trust in human
beings who often fail me. I desire to put my
trust in Christ alone—He who never fails.

Listen and Learn

I will instruct thee and teach thee in the way which
thou shalt go: I will guide thee with mine eye.

PSALM 32:8

To learn, you have to listen. Are you really listening to what God is trying to teach you? Whether it's reading the Bible, listening to a message at church, or receiving counsel from someone who is farther down the road of faith than you happen to be, there is always more to learn. Prepare your heart with prayer. Ask God to help you clearly understand what you need to learn and then act on what you hear.

Father God, please open my mind and my heart to
understand what You want me to learn. Give me wisdom
and energy to carry out the plans You have for me.

Godly Counsel

The mouth of the righteous speaketh wisdom,
and his tongue talketh of judgment.

PSALM 37:30

Want to run a marathon? Talk to those who've run one before. They know how to train, which shoes to buy, and what to expect when the big day arrives. The same is true if you want to go the distance with God. When you meet people who have followed God for many years, ask questions. Discover what they've learned, where they've struggled, and how they study the Bible. You may gain new friends, as well as godly counsel.

Lord, please bring people into my life who can offer
godly wisdom from a lifetime of trusting You.
Prepare my heart to accept their wisdom.

God-Honoring Life

So teach us to number our days,
that we may apply our hearts unto wisdom.

PSALM 90:12

Want to live life in a way that honors God? There are so many options it's hard to know what to do. But in Matthew 22:37–39, Jesus sums up the purpose of life by saying we're to love God and love others. Prayerfully weighing the choices before us against these two commands can help us make wise decisions. We don't know how long our lives will be, but with love as our goal, we're certain to use our time well.

Lord, let my life goals line up with Your goals for me—
to love You and to love others well. May I make
choices based on those goals alone.

Extraordinary Treasures

What man is he that desireth life,
and loveth many days, that he may see good?

PSALM 34:12

God is amazingly creative and incomparably loving. Having Someone like that design a plan for your life is an exciting prospect. God promises there are good things ahead for you. That promise is enough to make each morning feel like a chest filled with treasure just waiting to be opened. Greet each new day with expectation. Invite God to join you in your search for the extraordinary treasures He's scattered throughout even the most ordinary of days.

Before my feet hit the ground, remind me that You are
with me, Lord Jesus. Help me to see Your
blessings in each new day.

Connected

Turn thee unto me, and have mercy upon me;
for I am desolate and afflicted.

PSALM 25:16

In Genesis we read about creation. God declared everything He created "good," with one exception. God said it was not good for Adam to be alone. God designed people to be in relationships with each other and with Him. When you're feeling lonely, God agrees: It's not good. Ask God to bring a new friend your way and help you connect more deeply with those already in your life. But for right now, invite God to meet your deepest need.

Heavenly Father, please bring friends into my life
who can become good and healthy members
of my family. I trust You to meet my need
for healthy, thriving relationships.

God's Presence

*Unto thee, O my strength, will I sing: for God is
my defence, and the God of my mercy.*

PSALM 59:17

When you're feeling lonely, picture God beside you in the room. Talk to Him the way you would a dear friend. If praying aloud feels awkward, journal or write God a love note that you can tuck in your Bible. Read the book of Psalms. See what other people had to say to God when they felt the way you do right now. Remember, God is with you, whether you're aware of His presence or not.

*I ask again, Lord, that You open my eyes to spiritual
things. I feel alone, and I want to know that You
are near. Please show Yourself to me.*

Great Is His Love

For as the heaven is high above the earth,
so great is his mercy toward them that fear him.

PSALM 103:11

It's hard to grasp how deeply God cares for us, because our firsthand experience of love comes from relationships with imperfect people. But God's love is different. With God, we need never fear condemnation, misunderstanding, or rejection. He completely understands what we say and how we feel—and loves us without condition. Since God is never fickle or self-centered, we can risk opening up every part of our lives to Him. We can risk returning the love He so freely gives.

I love You, heavenly Father. I want to honor You with my
life and share every part of my heart with You.
I seek You with all my heart.

Before Time

But I am like a green olive tree in the house of God:
I trust in the mercy of God for ever and ever.

PSALM 52:8

How do you love someone you can't see, hear, or touch?
The same way you love an unborn child. You learn everything you can about what that child is like. You speak to it,
even though it doesn't speak back. When you finally meet
face-to-face, you find you're already in love. Yes, you can
love someone you cannot yet see. As for God, His love for
you transcends eternity. You're the child He's loved since
before there was time.

Lord, prepare my heart to live in relationship with You
all the days of my life. I love You, and I want to
learn how to show my love for You.

Shelter of Love

Surely goodness and mercy shall follow me all the days of my life: and I will dwell in the house of the LORD for ever.

PSALM 23:6

In old-fashioned melodramas and classic films, repentant scoundrels throw themselves on the mercy of the court. This means they know what they've done is wrong, there's no possible way they can make it right, and their only hope for redemption is to ask the court to extend what they don't deserve: mercy. God extends mercy to us each day. He's sentenced us to life—eternal life—and to the freedom to grow in the shelter of His love.

Hide me in Your shelter, Lord. I cannot thank You enough for taking my life and making it new. . . allowing me to live eternally with You.

Live, Love, Grow

When I said, My foot slippeth;
thy mercy, O LORD, held me up.

PSALM 94:18

There's safety in planting yourself in a recliner and interacting with the world via big-screen TV. No real relationships to let you down or challenge you to grow up. Nothing to risk, so no chance to fail. But nowhere in scripture do we see inaction as God's plan for our lives. We're designed to live, love, and grow. Along the way, we'll also fall. It's part of being human. God's mercy gives us the courage to risk trying again.

Father, I'm a little scared to carry out Your plans for
my life. Will You give me strength and courage
to do Your will? I need You every moment.

God's Artwork

He telleth the number of the stars;
he calleth them all by their names.

PSALM 147:4

Like a child who carefully chooses the silver crayon to draw the dog with stars for eyes, God's artwork is an expression of who He is. It displays His creativity, attention to detail, love of diversity, meticulous organization, and even His sense of humor. Taking time to contemplate the beauty and complexity of nature can help paint a clearer picture for you of what God is like. He's an artist, as well as a Father, Savior, and friend.

I love looking at Your handiwork, Lord.
Your creativity shows how amazing and real You
are. Help me to never take Your creation for granted.

Something from Nothing

By the word of the Lord were the heavens made;
and all the host of them by the breath of his mouth.

PSALM 33:6

Genesis tells us how God spoke nothing into something. But that "something" was not just anything. It was the divine artwork of creation. All of creation, from the tiniest microbe to the most expansive nebula, is wonderful in the fullest sense of the word. Take time to appreciate the wonder God has woven into the world. Take a walk in a park. Fill a vase with fresh flowers. Pet a puppy. Plant a petunia. Then, thank God.

Thank You for allowing us to spend time in Your
wonderful creation, Lord God! I'm so amazed by
You and Your divine artwork. Thank You, God!

His Time, His Way

Rest in the LORD, and wait patiently for him:
fret not thyself because of him who prospereth
in his way, because of the man who
bringeth wicked devices to pass.

PSALM 37:7

When we encounter conflict or injustice, we want resolution. We want relationships to be mended and wrongs to be made right. We want villains to pay and victims to heal. Now. Wanting this life to resemble heaven is a God-given desire. But the fact is, we're not home yet. If you're impatient for a situation to change, pray for perspective, do what you can, then trust God for resolution in His time and in His way.

Lord, please give me Your perspective while I'm here on earth. Some situations and conflicts simply baffle me. I lift my cares into Your loving, capable hands.

Part of God's Plan

Mine eyes fail for thy salvation,
and for the word of thy righteousness.

PSALM 119:123

In an age of microwave meals, instant access, and ATMs, patience is fast becoming a lost virtue. Heaven forbid we're forced to use dial-up instead of broadband! But waiting is part of God's plan. It takes time for babies to mature, for seasons to change, for fruit to ripen, and sometimes for prayers to be answered. Having to wait on God's timing reminds us that God is not our genie in a bottle. He's our sovereign Lord.

Help me to wait on Your plans and Your timing, Lord.
I often trudge ahead on my own, and that's
when I fail the most. I need You, Jesus.

Peace of Heart

Let them shout for joy, and be glad, that favour
my righteous cause: yea, let them say continually,
Let the LORD be magnified, which hath pleasure
in the prosperity of his servant.

PSALM 35:27

The peace God pours out on those who follow Him runs deeper than peace of mind. It overflows into peace of heart. As you trust God a little more each day, placing the things you cherish most in His loving hands, you will release a need to control, a tendency toward worry, and a fear for the future. In their place, you will discover the comfort of being cared for like a child being held in a parent's nurturing embrace.

Forgive me for my control issues, Lord. Help me to
trust You with each issue in my life, knowing
You are the source of all wisdom.

Place of Peace

Mercy and truth are met together;
righteousness and peace have kissed each other.

PSALM 85:10

When you follow God's lead and do what you know He wants you to do, you discover a place of peace. Outward struggles may continue, but inside you can relax. You've done what you could with what God has given you—and that's enough. Listen for God's whisper of, "Well done, my beautiful daughter." It's there. Rest in that place of peace and allow yourself to celebrate how far you've come and to anticipate what is still ahead.

Father, let my ears hear Your loving words.
Help me to relax in Your great love for me.
You've got this! What a great Dad You are.

Perseverance

Wait on the LORD: be of good courage, and he shall strengthen thine heart: wait, I say, on the LORD.

PSALM 27:14

Life is short, but some days seem to last forever. When you're facing a difficult day, don't face it alone. Take a good look at your exhaustion, anxiety, and fears. Picture entrusting them, one-by-one, into God's hands. Then take an objective look at what you need to do today. Invite God to join you as you take one step at a time in accomplishing what lies ahead. Throughout the day, remind yourself that God is right by your side.

Lord, I can't get through this day without You.
I want Your peace and love to guide each moment.
Remind me that I'm never alone.

One Day at a Time

Blessed is he whose transgression is forgiven,
whose sin is covered.

PSALM 32:1

It's hard to keep moving forward if you're dragging along baggage that weighs you down. God wants to help you discard what you don't need. Insecurity, guilt, shame, bad habits, past mistakes—leave them by the side of the road. Jesus has already paid the price for their removal. Once your past is truly behind you, you'll find it much easier to persevere. Tackling only one day at a time is downright doable with God's help.

Lord, help me to not allow people to toss baggage onto me
that You've already destroyed. I walk in the truth of who
You say I am. My past and my future are in Your hands.

God's Power

The LORD is my strength and song,
and is become my salvation.

PSALM 118:14

Moses parted the Red Sea. Peter walked upon the waves. David slaughtered a giant with a single stone. God's power was the force behind them all. How will God's power work through you? Perhaps you'll conquer an addiction, face your fear of public speaking, forgive what seems unforgivable, serve the homeless, or lead someone into a closer relationship with God. When God is honored through what you do, you can be sure His power is at work in you.

I know Your power is at work in me, Jesus!
I'm so amazed at how You choose to work
through me. Have Your way, Lord.

Mighty Power

Let them praise thy great
and terrible name; for it is holy.

PSALM 99:3

God's power is mightier than any created thing. After all, God simply spoke, and the power of His words brought everything else into existence. That kind of power can move mountains—or change lives. God's power is at work to help you accomplish things you never would have dreamed of doing on your own. Whatever God leads you to do, He will provide the power you need to see it through.

I know that You fully equip me to do everything
You ask of me, Lord God. Help me to step
out in faith, trusting Your heart.

Reason for Praise

For a day in thy courts is better than a thousand.

PSALM 84:10

What words would you use to describe God? Loving. Forgiving. Powerful. Creative. Wise. Merciful. Eternal. Glorious. Dependable. Truthful. Compassionate. Faithful. Friend. Father. Savior. Every word you can think of is reason for praise. When you pray, share more than a list of requests with God. Tell God how much He means to you. Choose one attribute of God and tell Him how that character trait has made a difference in your life.

You are the everlasting God, Creator of all,
Savior of the world, and friend of my soul.
What a comfort those truths are to me.

Pray, Sing, Dance

*O sing unto the L*ORD *a new song;*
for he hath done marvellous things.

PSALM 98:1

Consider the wide variety of ways we can tell people we love how wonderful they are: send flowers, hire a skywriter, write a poem, proclaim it via Twitter, send a card, share a hug. The list goes on and on. The same is true for the ways we can praise God. We can pray, sing, dance, write our own psalm, use our God-given talents and resources in ways that honor Him. What novel way will you praise God today?

I pray that You would show me how to use my whole
body to praise You, Lord. Move me outside
my comfort zone to worship You.

Conversation of Prayer

But I have trusted in thy mercy; my heart shall rejoice in thy salvation. I will sing unto the LORD, because he hath dealt bountifully with me.

PSALM 13:5-6

When we pray, we expect things to happen—and they do. Inviting the Creator of the universe to be intimately involved in the details of our day is a mysterious and miraculous undertaking. But prayer isn't a tool. It's a conversation. God is not our almighty personal planner, helping us manage our lives more efficiently. He's Someone who loves us. When you pray, remember you're speaking to Someone who enjoys you, as well as takes care of you.

Lord, please forgive me for treating You like a personal assistant instead of the Creator of all and the lover of my soul. I want to show my love for You.

He Draws Near

The LORD is nigh unto all them that call upon him,
to all that call upon him in truth.

PSALM 145:18

God is always attentive, listening for the voice of His children. Like a mother who hears her child's cry through a baby monitor in the middle of the night, God acts on what He hears. He draws near to comfort, protect, and guide. Never hesitate to call on Him—anytime, anywhere. He isn't bothered by your questions or put off by an overflow of emotion. What touches your life touches Him.

Your Word tells me that when I draw close to You,
You will draw close to me. I come, Lord Jesus.
Please be close to me.

Together

My soul thirsteth for God, for the living God:
when shall I come and appear before God?

PSALM 42:2

When you're in love, you long to be with the one who has captured your heart. It makes little difference if you're sharing a sumptuous sunset dinner cruise or toiling together to complete a mundane task. What matters is that you're together. When we first get to know God, we long to spend time with Him because of what He provides. But the longer we spend in His presence, the more we desire Him simply because of who He is.

Lord, You are continually healing and restoring my soul.
I praise You for that. I love You, God. I long to
know You more and more.

Blessed Assurance

In my distress I called upon the Lord, and cried unto
my God: he heard my voice out of his temple,
and my cry came before him, even into his ears.

PSALM 18:6

It can be difficult to picture yourself in the presence of Someone you cannot see. But the Bible assures us God is near. His Spirit not only surrounds us, but also moves within us. When God's presence feels far away, remember that what you feel is not an accurate gauge of the truth. Read the Psalms to remind yourself that others have felt the way you do. Then, follow the psalmists' example. Continue praising God and moving ahead in faith.

Lord, will You give me a picture of who You are?
Something to see in my mind's eye that lines up with
the truth of who You are. . . I want to see You, Lord.

Protection

The angel of the LORD encampeth round about them
that fear him, and delivereth them.

PSALM 34:7

In the Bible we read about angelic beings who act as God's messengers and warriors. Far from cute little cherubs who do nothing more than pluck harps on cotton-ball clouds, we meet angels who yield swords and have ferocious, lion like faces. But the message they continually tell God's children is, "Be not afraid." When you're in need of protection, remember there's more going on than is visible to the eye. God's angels have your back.

I don't understand the unseen world, but I trust the truth
of Your Word. You tell me that You send Your angels
to protect me. All praise and honor to You, Lord.

A Safe Haven

But let all those that put their trust in thee rejoice:
let them ever shout for joy, because thou defendest them:
let them also that love thy name be joyful in thee.

PSALM 5:11

In the Old Testament, God designates cities of refuge. These were places where people who'd accidentally killed someone could flee. Here they'd be safe from the vengeance of angry relatives until they'd received a fair trial or had proven their innocence. God is a place of refuge for His children. No matter what happens, you're under God's protection. Flee to Him in prayer when you feel under attack. God provides a safe haven where truth will be brought to light.

You are my refuge, my ever-present help in times
of trouble. I seek You, Lord. Protect me from
the enemy's attacks on my life.

Share Your Heart

Who satisfieth thy mouth with good things;
so that thy youth is renewed like the eagle's.

PSALM 103:5

What do you need today? Whether it's the finances to pay a fast-approaching bill or the courage to have a difficult conversation with a friend, God wants to provide what you need. Share your heart with Him. But before you rush off to other things, sit quietly and listen. God may reveal how you can work with Him to meet that need. He may also want to help you share with others what He's already so generously provided.

Teach me how to listen to You, heavenly Father.
And then please give me Your heart and strength
to carry out what You ask of me.

Countless Gifts

Who covereth the heaven with clouds,
who prepareth rain for the earth, who maketh
grass to grow upon the mountains.

PSALM 147:8

God provides for us in so many ways that it's easy to take them for granted. The fact that the sun rises each morning, encouraging crops to grow, or that our heart takes its next beat and our lungs their next breath are just a few of the countless gifts we receive from God's almighty hand. As you go through the day, consider the big and little ways God meets your needs. Then take time at the day's end to give thanks.

Your provision for me is abundant when I trust You
to take care of me. I fail when I try to meet my
own needs. I surrender to You, Lord.

Created for a Purpose

I will cry unto God most high; unto God that
performeth all things for me.

PSALM 57:2

A beautiful woman like yourself was created for more than decoration. You were created for a purpose. Your purpose is not a specific job God has designated for you to accomplish. It's more like a unique spot He's designed for you to fill. God is working with you, encouraging you to grow into this "sweet spot." As you learn to lean on Him, God will help you discover the true joy and significance that come from simply being "you."

Thank You, God, for the time and location You've placed
me in—my piece of this planet. I offer myself
and all I have to You to do as You will.

How Will You Answer?

The counsel of the LORD standeth for ever,
the thoughts of his heart to all generations.

PSALM 33:11

In Exodus we read how God called Moses to lead the children of Israel out of slavery in Egypt. Moses said yes to the leading but no to the public speaking. Moses' "no" didn't prevent God's plan from taking place. God used Aaron, Moses' brother, to be His spokesperson in Moses' stead. God's purpose and plan for this world will happen. God has given you the free will to say whether you'll take part or not. What will your answer be?

I know Your plans and purposes prevail, Lord God.
I want to say yes to all that You ask of me.
Please give me strength and wisdom. Thank You.

Make a Date

*Delight thyself also in the LORD: and he shall
give thee the desires of thine heart.*

PSALM 37:4

Sometimes, drawing close to God can feel like an eternal
to-do list instead of a relationship. If praying, reading scripture, going to church, or serving others begins to feel like
just another task, don't settle for checking them off your
list. That's ritual, not relationship. Instead, make a date
with God. Set up a time and place. Then simply talk and
listen. Focus on who God is. Take the time to fall in love
with Him all over again.

*God, I want to fall wholeheartedly in love
with You. Will You lead me in this process?
Open my heart to hear from You.*

Lifting Up in Prayer

The LORD shall increase you more and more,
you and your children.

PSALM 115:14

Praying for the people you care about is one way of loving them. When you pray for them, you invite God to work in their lives. What more loving gift could there be than that? But prayer also softens your own heart toward those you're praying for. With God's help, you feel their needs more deeply, understand their motivations more clearly, and can forgive their faults more completely. There's no downside to lifting those you love up in prayer.

Lord, I bring my loved ones before You—those who I
thoroughly enjoy and those who are difficult
to love. Show me how to love them well.

Renewal

For his anger endureth but a moment; in his favour
is life: weeping may endure for a night,
but joy cometh in the morning.

PSALM 30:5

Renewal isn't taking a deep breath, smiling through gritted teeth, and muscling your way through today. Renewal is a kind of rebirth. It's letting the past fall from your shoulders and welcoming hope back into your heart. Renewal is a work of the Spirit, not a state of mind or act of the will. It's joining hands with God and moving forward together, expectant and refreshed. Are you ready to release whatever's holding you back and reach out to God?

God, I ask You to renew my heart. I come to You to be
fully restored in You alone. I bring all of me.
Please fill me with Your presence.

Like New

Create in me a clean heart, O God;
and renew a right spirit within me.

PSALM 51:10

Laundry is an ongoing process. You wear clothes, soil them, and then wash them over and over again. But even after washing, clothes are never really new again. Don't confuse God's forgiveness with a trip to the Laundromat. When God forgives you, He doesn't just wash away your sins; He gives you a totally clean heart. There's no dull residue or faint stains of rebellion. You're renewed—not reused or recycled or "just like new." Your heart's new. Again.

The old me is gone, and the fully restored me
is here because of You, Jesus. Your work
on the cross has made me brand-new!

Respect

But as for me, I will come into thy house in the multitude
of thy mercy: and in thy fear will I worship
toward thy holy temple.

PSALM 5:7

It's true God is our Friend. But He's more than our BFF.
God is our sovereign Lord and King. He's the One who
initiated this implausibly intimate relationship, Creator
with creation. But God's overwhelming love for us should
not lull us into a familiarity that disregards reverence and
respect. There will come a time when every knee will bow
to Him. Until that day, may our awe and esteem continue
to grow right along with our love.

Father, I want to honor You in Your holiness and glory.
You alone deserve all my praise and worship.
I respect You and lift You high!

Respect with Love

Come, ye children, hearken unto me:
I will teach you the fear of the LORD.

PSALM 34:11

Consider the teachers and leaders who have helped draw you closer to God. These people are worthy of your thanks and prayers, but they're also worthy of your respect. The Bible tells us God is the power behind those in authority. But these people are still human. They make mistakes. They make decisions we don't always agree with. We aren't asked to blindly follow, but we are asked to love. Respect is one side of that love.

Father, please help me to love and respect those
in authority over me. And when I don't agree,
give me wisdom to share my heart
when the time is right.

Rest

*He maketh me to lie down in green pastures:
he leadeth me beside the still waters. He restoreth
my soul: he leadeth me in the paths of
righteousness for his name's sake.*

PSALM 23:2-3

God created the world in six days. Then He took a day to sit back and enjoy all of the good things He'd done. The Bible tells us God doesn't tire or sleep, but even He knew the value of a time-out. If you're weary, or simply trying to keep up with a hectic schedule, let God lead you beside quiet waters. Look back over what you and God have accomplished together. Rejoice, then rest so God can restore.

*Father, I come to You with all my burdens and activities,
and I ask You to give me rest. Your Word tells me
that in You, I will find rest for my soul.*

Rest in Him

He that dwelleth in the secret place of the most
High shall abide under the shadow of the Almighty.

PSALM 91:1

Picture a hammock in the shade of two leafy trees, swaying gently in the breeze. Now picture yourself nestled there, eyes closed, totally relaxed. This is what it's like to rest in the shadow of the Almighty. Knowing that God holds you tenderly in His hand, offering protection, comfort, and grace, allows you to let go of your fears and concerns. God knows about them all. Rest in the fact that scripture says nothing is impossible with God.

I dwell in the shelter of the Most High God. I rest in
the shadow of Your wings, Lord. Hide me in
that safe shelter, as I rest in You.

Rewards

Moreover by them is thy servant warned:
and in keeping of them there is great reward.

PSALM 19:11

Doing the right thing comes with its own rewards. Whether it's the actual Ten Commandments or other teachings found in scripture, following what God says is right points the way toward loving relationships and a balanced life. Obedience comes with the added bonus of a guilt-free conscience and the knowledge that we're living a life that pleases the Father who so deeply loves us. These are rewards that won't tarnish with the passing of time.

Lord, help me to follow You and make choices that honor You. I want to serve You well out of my deep love for You.

Worth Rewarding

Also unto thee, O Lord, belongeth mercy:
for thou renderest to every man according to his work.

PSALM 62:12

Revelation, the final book of the Bible, gives us a peek at what heaven will be like. One thing we discover is that we'll be rewarded for what we've done here on earth. But instead of putting these rewards on display in our heavenly mansions, we're told that the elders in the group will lay these rewards before God's throne. That's truly where they belong. God is the One who enables and inspires us to do what's worth rewarding.

All my rewards and trophies and successes. . . I lay them
before You, Jesus. They mean nothing compared to
the greatness of having a relationship with You.

Righteousness

Thy righteousness is like the great mountains;
thy judgments are a great deep: O LORD,
thou preservest man and beast.

PSALM 36:6

God's goodness is more than Him playing "nice." God's goodness is an extension of His righteousness. Since God is loving and just, the morally virtuous thing for Him to do is provide His children with a balance of mercy and discipline, guidelines and grace. That's why a price had to be paid for our sins. God's righteousness demanded it. But God's love allowed Jesus to pay a debt we couldn't afford to pay on our own.

It is so hard to fathom that You see me as righteous,
heavenly Father! I know this righteousness You see
came at a great price. I'm so thankful, Jesus!

Righteousness in Action

Blessed are they that keep judgment,
and he that doeth righteousness at all times.

PSALM 106:3

Living a moral life, a life that honors God and those around you, is righteousness in action. It's the opposite of self-righteousness. That's a life where you justify doing what you deem right, regardless of whether God agrees with your assessment. Righteousness, however, reflects God's own character. It shows you truly are His child. Your actions are not swayed by emotion, peer pressure, or personal gain. You do what's right simply because it's the right thing to do.

Lord, help me to live a life that honors You above all.
Show me how to honor and love the people
You've placed in my life too.

Sacrifice

*The sacrifices of God are a broken spirit: a broken
and a contrite heart, O God, thou wilt not despise.*

PSALM 51:17

Sacrifice can be motivated by love, necessity, or obligation.
God asks only for sacrifices motivated by our love for Him.
That doesn't mean they don't come at a price. When we
place our own pride on the altar and acknowledge that
God is in control and we are not, it can be painful. But
it's like the pain that follows a much-needed surgery. It's
a precursor to healing. What we give up out of love, we're
better off without.

*I bring my whole self to You, Lord. Please cut out
the parts in me that are prideful and arrogant.
I want to choose You in each situation.*

Sacrifice of Thanks

Offer unto God thanksgiving;
and pay thy vows unto the most High.

PSALM 50:14

In the Old Testament, we read about God's people offering sacrifices to pay the price for their rebellion against God. In the New Testament, these sacrifices disappear—except one. When Jesus willingly went to the cross for us, He became the ultimate sacrifice. His death paid for the wrongs we've done once and for all. Each time we choose to follow God instead of our own hearts, we offer a sacrifice of thanks in return for all Jesus has done.

You paid the price for my freedom once and for all,
Lord. I am amazed at what You've done. I praise
and thank You for this overwhelming gift of love.

Satisfaction

O satisfy us early with thy mercy;
that we may rejoice and be glad all our days.

PSALM 90:14

Each morning when you rise, take time to turn your eyes toward the Son. Take a fresh look at what Jesus has done out of love for you. Recall what you've been forgiven and the many blessings you've received. Consider how following in Jesus' footsteps has changed the direction of your life—and will change the day ahead. Allow gratitude to wash over you anew. There's no greater satisfaction than seeing your life in the light of God's great love.

Father, instill in me the habit of praising You every
morning upon waking. I'm so thankful for the gift of
a new day. Remind me of Your presence in every moment.

Needy Hearts

Thou openest thine hand,
and satisfiest the desire of
every living thing.

PSALM 145:16

Our hearts are needy. They cry out for love, relief, pleasure, and purpose. They cry out for what they see on TV. Only God can quiet their relentless cry. That's because God is what they're actually crying out for. As we open our hearts more fully to God, we'll see more clearly that our needs are being met. What's more, we'll notice that our desires are changing, aligning themselves more and more with God's own.

Lord, I ask that You would align my heart with Your
will. Draw me closer to You, as You continue to
meet each one of my needs.

Safe and Secure

For the word of the LORD is right;
and all his works are done in truth.

God's power is limitless. That's tough to comprehend. But knowing God has the ability to care for us in any and all circumstances is not the true reason why we can feel safe and secure in His presence. Being in the presence of a beefy bodyguard only feels safe if you know that person is trustworthy, if you know he's on your side. God is on your side, fighting for you. You can trust His strength and His love.

Forgive me for when I've doubted Your power, Lord.
I've seen You at work, and I know I can trust You with
every detail of my life, both the big and small!

Before You Call

*Thou art my hiding place; thou shalt preserve me
from trouble; thou shalt compass me about
with songs of deliverance.*

PSALM 32:7

Having an alarm system installed in your home can give
you a sense of security. If someone tries to break in, you
can trust that help is immediately on the way. God is a
24-hour security system. When you call, He's there. But
the truth is, God's there even before you call. He won't
hesitate to step in to protect you, even if you're unaware
of the danger you're in.

*I am safely tucked away in Your hand, Almighty God.
You are my loving and unfailing heavenly Father.
I love You, Lord. I'm safe in You.*

Serving God

*Rejoice the soul of thy servant: for unto thee,
O Lord, do I lift up my soul.*

PSALM 86:4

The people we love, we serve. If a friend's car breaks down, we give her a lift. If she's ill, we make her family a meal. We may use the word *help* instead of *serve*, but the result is the same. Love leads us to act. As our love for God grows, so will our desire to serve Him. One way we serve God is to care for those He loves. Ask God whom He'd like you to serve today.

*I am grateful to be a part of Your family, God.
I want to serve my brothers and sisters out of love.
Show me what You need me to do next.*

Saying "Yes"

Serve the LORD with gladness: come
before his presence with singing.

PSALM 100:2

We live in a needy world. People around the globe need
food and medical care. People in our city need shelter. Our
church needs volunteers to serve in the nursery. We can't
fill every need. And God doesn't expect us to. We have
limited time, energy, and resources. That's why prayer is
such an important part of serving. Only with God's help
will we have the wisdom and courage to say yes or no to
the opportunities that surround us.

Lord, please give me wisdom to say yes or no when
I'm asked to do good things. I know I can't do
it all. I want to do what is best.

Savor Today

When I remember thee upon my bed,
and meditate on thee in the night watches.

PSALM 63:6

Close your day in a wonderful way by spending it in your Father's arms. Instead of allowing your thoughts to race ahead toward tomorrow, take time to savor today. Regardless of whether it's been a day you'll long remember or one you'd rather forget, ask God to help you recall what matters. Thank Him for His loving care. Ask forgiveness for any moments when you turned your back on Him. Then relax and rest, knowing He's near.

I'm not promised tomorrow, so I thank You for this day,
Lord. I won't stress about what lies ahead, because only
You know exactly what will happen. I trust in You.

Worth Dreaming

Thou tellest my wanderings: put thou my tears
into thy bottle: are they not in thy book?

PSALM 56:8

Insomnia can feel like a curse. Your mind races and your body aches for rest. When sleep is elusive, rest in God. Set your mind on Him, instead of on what lies heavy on your heart. Meditate on a single verse of scripture, allowing the truth of God's words to release the tension from your body and the muddle in your mind. Curl up in the crook of God's arm and let Him draw you toward dreams worth dreaming.

When I'm awake at night, I lift my heart to You, Lord.
There is a reason when sleep eludes me, and so
I share my thoughts and feelings with You.

Your Words

Let the words of my mouth, and the meditation of my
heart, be acceptable in thy sight, O Lord,
my strength, and my redeemer.

Psalm 19:14

God hears the words you speak. He even hears the ones that remain unsaid anywhere other than your mind. Sometimes it's hard to get words past your lips. It's difficult to apologize, comfort someone who's hurting, or try to untangle miscommunication in a relationship. It can even be difficult to say, "I love you." With God's help, you can say what needs to be said. Ask God to help you speak the right words at the right time.

Let my words build others up according to their needs,
Lord. Help me to choose my words wisely
and speak them at the right time.

A Welcome Source

Set a watch, O LORD, before my mouth;
keep the door of my lips.

PSALM 141:3

The words we speak have power. They can hurt or heal, repel or attract. They also provide a fairly accurate barometer as to what's going on in our hearts. If you find words slipping out that you wish you could take back, return to the source. Ask God to reveal what's going on in your heart. With God's help, your words can become a welcome source of comfort and encouragement to those around you.

Reveal my heart as I speak, Lord. Convict me of the ways
that I might not be honoring You or those around me.
Realign my heart to do Your will.

Spiritual Growth

*Be still, and know that I am God: I will be exalted
among the heathen, I will be exalted in the earth.*

PSALM 46:10

What season of spiritual growth are you in? Springtime's early bud of new love? Basking in summer's sunshine, growing by fruitful leaps and bounds? Knee-deep in autumn, with remnants of your old life falling like dead leaves around your feet? Or praying your way through winter, where God and that joy of first love seem far away? Whatever season you're in, remember: God's the only One who can make something grow. Trust His timing and watch for fruit.

---

*Father, I'm so thankful for the different seasons of life.
Each season has its purpose. I wait patiently through
difficulty, knowing that a new season of growth is coming.*

One-of-a-Kind Adventure

Blessed is the man whose strength is in thee;
in whose heart are the ways of them.

PSALM 84:5

You're embarking on a lifelong spiritual journey. It's a pilgrimage that will follow a different path than that of anyone else who has ever desired to grow closer to God. The prayers you pray, how quickly you mature, the battles you fight, the challenges you overcome, and the person you become will all add up to a one-of-a-kind adventure. Look to God instead of comparing yourself to others to gauge how far you've come and what direction you're headed next.

Thank You for the path You've set before me, heavenly Father. I trust that You are with me each step of the way. Guide me in the way of truth and love.

A Fresh Start

The L<small>ORD</small> rewarded me according to my righteousness;
according to the cleanness of my hands hath
he recompensed me.

PSALM 18:20

Picture your life as a jigsaw puzzle. You've been trying to put it together for years, with limited success. Some pieces are lost or bent beyond recognition. What's worse is that you have no idea what the final picture is supposed to be. Want a do-over? God offers you one. Simply admit you need His help. Then hand the pieces of your life over to Him. God will help you create a life that's beautiful, significant, and complete.

My past looks rather messy, I admit. I want You to be the
designer of my life, Lord—today and every day to
come. Make something beautiful out of me.

Set Free

Therefore hath the LORD recompensed me according
to my righteousness, according to the cleanness
of my hands in his eyesight.

PSALM 18:24

God can rewrite your life's story line. It's true that what's done is done—God won't change the past—but He can change how you see it. He can reveal how He has woven themes of redemption and blessing throughout what once looked hopeless. He can also change how the past affects you. Through His power, God can free you from the bondage of bad habits and past mistakes. As for the future, that's a fresh page. What will God and you cowrite?

I praise You for rewriting my story, Father! You are freeing
me, day by day, moment by moment! You are making
something beautiful out of the ashes of my past.

Spiritual Strength

Cast thy burden upon the LORD, and he shall sustain thee: he shall never suffer the righteous to be moved.

PSALM 55:22

You can gain physical strength by heading to the gym. However, spiritual strength is what you need to carry you through life. Instead of lifting weights, lift your eyes and prayers toward heaven. Stretch your compassion by reaching out to those around you in love. Get your heart pumping as you push beyond your own limitations and rely more completely on God. Through it all, God will be your strength as well as your personal trainer.

You are my strength, Lord. I come to You for all my needs—physical, emotional, and spiritual. You meet each one as I bring them to You.

The Strength You Need

Because of his strength will I wait upon thee: for God is my defence. The God of my mercy shall prevent me: God shall let me see my desire upon mine enemies.

PSALM 59:9-10

Some people believe that if they follow God, life will be trouble-free. Jesus doesn't seem to agree. In John 16:33, Jesus says, "In the world ye shall have tribulation." But Jesus doesn't leave it at that. He continues, "But be of good cheer; I have overcome the world." Don't be surprised when struggle comes, but don't lose heart either. God will provide the strength you need when you need it to help you overcome whatever comes your way.

There is definitely trouble here on earth, but I know You've overcome, Lord Jesus. I won't despair, because I know You are with me always.

Success That Matters

It's tempting to do what we want—while asking God to bless what we do. But a "please bless my efforts" prayer is not a rubber stamp of God's approval or our success. Regardless of what's on your agenda today, invite God to be part of your plans—from the conception stage right through to the celebration of its completion. God will help you align your motives and methods with His own and succeed in the ways that matter most.

*Instead of asking You just to bless my plans, Father,
help me to seek Your will for what You want
me to do in the first place!*

A Humble Heart

*And he shall be like a tree planted by the rivers of water,
that bringeth forth his fruit in his season; his leaf also
shall not wither; and whatsoever he doeth shall prosper.*

PSALM 1:3

How do you measure success? By your title? Your weight?
Your net worth? The opinion of others? God's measure of
success has little to do with accolades, appearance, acqui-
sitions, or admiration. According to the Bible, the key to
real success is love. The more we love God and others, the
more successful we are at fulfilling what God has planned
for our lives. Want to be a truly successful woman? Serve
others with a humble heart.

*I want to be known for my love, Lord. My love for You—
and for everyone around me. Help me to love wisely,
from a place of dependence on You.*

Thankfulness

It is a good thing to give thanks unto the LORD,
and to sing praises unto thy name, O Most High.

PSALM 92:1

It used to be considered proper etiquette to send a hand-written thank-you note for every gift you received. Consider how high a stack of note cards you'd need if you formally thanked God for every gift He's given. Sending a thank-you via prayer or singing God's praises are the most common ways God's children express their gratitude to Him. But don't let that stop you from getting creative. What new way can you thank God today?

How can I say thanks in a way that shows my love
for You, Lord? Show me new ways to bless
Your name. I'm so thankful!

Surge of Gratitude

For I have kept the ways of the LORD,
and have not wickedly departed from my God.

PSALM 18:21

The phrase "Thank God!" has lost much of its meaning these days. People use it interchangeably with expressions such as, "Wow!" "Thank goodness!" or "I really lucked out!" That's because people feel a surge of gratitude when good things happen to them, but not all of them are certain where they should direct their thanks. You've caught a glimpse of God's goodness. You know who is behind the blessings you receive. Don't hesitate to say, "Thank God!" and mean it.

I will thank You, God, for all the many blessings
in my life. You give and take away, Lord.
Blessed be Your name. Thank You, God!

Train of Thought

*Thou hast proved mine heart; thou hast visited me in
the night; thou hast tried me, and shalt find nothing.*

PSALM 17:3

When your mind wanders, where does it go? In your most
unguarded moments, when you're no longer focused on
deadlines and demands, what you think about is a strong
indicator of what matters most to you. Pay attention to where
your train of thought leads. Is it a direction you really want
to go? If you find your mind traveling roads that draw you
away from God, set your thoughts back on track toward
what's truly worth focusing on.

*Show me what it means to take every thought captive
to You, Jesus. When my mind goes blank, let it reset
on You. I give You full access to my thoughts.*

Turn Your Thoughts

*If I should count them, they are more in number
than the sand: when I awake, I am still with thee.*

PSALM 139:18

Trying to comprehend an infinite God with a finite brain
can leave you feeling small. That's okay. Compared to God,
we are. But when we balance the fact that a God too big
for our brains to hold cares for us with a love so deep that
nothing, absolutely nothing, can come between us, we find
peace, as well as perspective. Turn your thoughts toward
God, and your heart can't help but follow.

*I'm in awe of Your greatness, God. You are the all-
powerful God of Creation; and yet You are so
good to me. I give You my heart and my life.*

In God We Trust

*Some trust in chariots, and some in horses: but we will
remember the name of the LORD our God.*

PSALM 20:7

In the United States our currency proclaims, "In God We
Trust." That's easier said than done. It can be tempting to
trust more in the money this motto is printed on than in
God Himself. That's because trusting God means trusting
Someone we cannot see. It's like trusting an invisible chair
to hold your weight. You may believe it's there, but actually
sitting down takes faith. When your trust wavers, recall
God's faithfulness to you. Then step out in faith—and sit.

*I trust in Your name, God Almighty. You are Lord of all
the earth, Creator of the Universe, and still You know
when a sparrow falls. I adore You, Lord!*

Scripture Index